Berdeo

I hope you enjoy

Serenity: Aging With Dignity, Lving with Grace

8 STEPS TO HELP YOU OVERCOME ADVERSITY AND FIND PEACE OF MIND AND PROSPERITY IN THE SECOND HALF OF LIFE

© David H. Brady, MFA

Warmly

David Brady

CHAPTER TWO

My Generation   32

CHAPTER THREE

Time Flies When You Are Having Fun!   46

PART TWO

CHAPTER FOUR

There Is a Solution 53

CHAPTER FIVE

How To Work the Steps 58

CHAPTER SIX

I Believe 70

CHAPTER SEVEN

I Am Ready To Be Changed 82

CHAPTER EIGHT

I Decide To Be Changed 93

CHAPTER NINE

I Forgive   115

CHAPTER TEN

I Ask   132

CHAPTER ELEVEN

I Give Thanks 152

CHAPTER TWELVE

I Dedicate My Life 161

EPILOGUE

July 25, 2016

ACKNOWLEDGMENTS

I would like to thank my long-suffering family and friends who've all pitched in to help me.

A very special thanks to my business associate Sonny Goldstein and the incredible help he's been.

Thanks, Bev, for your patience and kindness.

A special thanks to Debbie Brand for your tireless efforts to reconstruct my manuscript.

Thanks to Tierney Ness and her good friend and trusty sailing partner, Barry Devonald, for your help on the early drafts of this manuscript.

I want to thank my oldest friends in the world, Mike O'Shea and Brian Rogers, for your undying support and kindness.

Thanks to my pals Kumar, Bert, Peter, and Tom, and Dr. Mike for being willing to give me honest feedback. Thanks to my new Master Mind partners, Mike, Barb, Jey, Carolynne, and Roy.

A very special thanks to my old friends Alan

Vogeler, George Flak, and Richard Landry.

FOREWORD

In the late spring of 2013, I was faced with one of the most difficult situations of my adult life. It appeared that in the first week of July, there was a chance I could lose everything I'd worked so hard to build up in the previous 30 years.

After having driven non-stop from Florida to Toronto in 30 hours I sustained a catastrophic brain injury in a bizarre and totally unexpected event. I was assaulted by a young man who was suffering from severe mental illness. I'd been asked on my drive back to Toronto to see if I could help him. Clearly, I could not.

While in a state of shock, and not really knowing what I was doing, I ended up driving for another two hours to try and get to my house in Eastern Ontario, across from Up State New York, where I felt I would be safe, only to end up in a hospital, where they diagnosed me with a concussion.

My face and skull showed significant trauma. As a result of that incident, I had brain damage that would dramatically change every aspect of my life. It would impair my ability to do the work I had done my entire career. That incident left me wondering how I would overcome these challenges. The bottom line was that this assault altered the direction of my life permanently.

What transpired three years after the initial assault was that the injury I sustained damaged my ability to create new projects and close new business. I am thankful to say that up until that point I had had an amazing career and great success in television production, working with my own company to produce a variety of popular shows. One of these was *Doc Zone.* In fact, our last CBC production was "Super Volcano, Yellowstone's Fury" for *Doc Zone* and was the highest rated production for 2013. It played in the United States on the Smithsonian Channel in 2014. *Doc Zone* was an idea my brother Jim suggested to me. It is the strand that is analogous to the "brass ring" for independent producers of documentaries in Canada, and the CBC is the world's second largest public broadcaster after the BBC.

Two of our other documentaries in late 2012

and early 2013 were rated in the top three for the year. In 2011, our series *Yonge Street, Toronto Rock & Roll Stories* aired on Bravo and CTV2 and garnered significant critical acclaim and awards. We also started this series in early 2009. Also, our other 2009 production, *The Gangster Next Door,* aired in 2011 and was one of CBC *Doc* Zone's top three rated shows for that year.

It seemed that I was competent as a producer. What I couldn't do, as I noted above, was "close" new business. And that was the most important part of my job. It is why I had the title producer and executive producer on over 130 episodes of primetime drama, comedies, docudramas, and documentaries and four feature films. My company had the privilege of producing for such studios as United Artists, Disney, and Zoetrope Studios.

This experience got me thinking. How many other people, or those of us who are "Baby Boomers," had been blindsided by some event that they didn't see coming? Would you know what to do if you had a life altering illness, accident, or totally unexpected event happen to you, one that you had no control over?

In my own case I did not. I now have firsthand knowledge and experience of what someone with Alzheimer's confronts when I ended up losing eighty percent of my memory.

I was physically impaired for several months and had ongoing emotional trauma. I would end up suffering from clinical depression, something I had avoided my whole life in spite of my own challenging upbringing in a violent alcoholic home.

What I've come to realize from this event is that life is often very unfair. Here I was trying to be of service and help someone, only to sustain a major life altering injury. But, then, as time went by I began to see that often every adversity carries within it the seed to a greater good. If I had not experienced this event, I would not have written this or my book Success: Reflections On Money, Sex and Power. I had already begun to write Survival: Transforming Childhood Trauma, which also was incredibly therapeutic process of letting go of the trauma of my childhood.

When I can let go of self-pity, when I can let go of resentment and anger, I can change the direction of my life from a negative perspective to a positive one.

That is why I wrote this book. To share my journey of overcoming this adversity and striving to find my real purpose in my second half of life. But change takes time. And, I'm an impatient guy.

I'm grateful to say that as a result of having met a wonderful physician, Dr. John Thornton in Toronto, who works with people who've suffered brain injuries, I started to heal. I also discovered and began using the Eight Steps of Master Mind, a program created by the late Jack Boland (a Unity Minister). I wondered if I would ever be able to find real meaning and purpose in my life. I was willing to do whatever was needed to be done so that I could be really happy again. I believed from the bottom of my heart that I would be able to solve both the emotional and financial issues that were facing me after this unfortunate incident.

Dr. Thornton emphasized that in addition to traditional medication I might want to examine universal spiritual principles to assist me in the healing of my injury. So, employing dedication as well as the Eight Steps as the tools of transformation, I set about to restore myself to wholeness and to find new meaning and purpose in my life.

Please don't let the term "Master Mind Principle" throw you off. A good friend of mine pointed out that the phrase has a great deal of energy and emotion — both negative and positive — assigned to it. The term was coined in the early 20th century by the late great Napoleon Hill, one of the forerunners of the human potential movement. In the context of this book, it is simply a way of denoting the concept of being able to access the "Divine Intelligence of the Universe or Spark of the Creator's Consciousness."

This book is not suggesting a religious solution, but rather one spiritual in nature. It's whatever you conceive to be the "Divine Mind" or God, as you understand God to be. This book is not trying to convince or convert anyone to any specific theology. But it borrows heavily from other spiritual movements that have emerged over the last several centuries. If you look around, you will soon realize that there are very few guides or how-to manuals that speak to these major life-altering transitions. No one tells you how to shift from a busy, active professional life to one where you have to cope with events like an unexpected illness or life-changing injury. What about the loss of a partner, the end of a marriage, or facing our own death?

What about the supposed "golden years"? There is absolutely no instruction booklet on how to handle the inevitable crises that are certain to arise over time. Banks, financial institutions, and insurance companies like to talk to us about our finances, but what about family relations, business relations, and lifelong friendships? What do we do if we find ourselves at odds with those closest to us, or we're on the outs with family members we've not spoken to for decades? For those of us who are further along in life, we do need to clean up these relationships before we die so we can have real peace of mind and real happiness in our later years. No one wants to leave the planet in a state of discord with his or her family. We are all going to reach the departure lounge — one day. Will you be ready?

Most importantly, this book will examine how we could live our lives in such a way that allows us to find a way to cope, stay happy, be productive, and create some purpose in life. Especially if we encounter some unexpected difficulties or challenges.

These were all the thoughts and questions racing through my mind in that late spring and early summer of 2013. At times I felt hopeful, at other times hopeless. I cried a lot over many weeks. I felt very alone and afraid. By 2014, it occurred to me that I might have to put my house in the country up for sale, because I had gone over one year with no new projects to produce. I slowly kept downsizing my company and burning through a lot of cash to keep the doors open and my staff employed. But one by one they had left, because they knew I didn't have the resources to keep going. I was facing some very big challenges. I don't wish to offend anyone with some of the information here, and hopefully you won't find what is being shared in bad taste. But this is what happened to me. That said, I will strive to be rigorously honest with you as I describe the process I came up with to solve my financial, emotional, and spiritual challenges that came about as a result of my injury. If I can find a way to be of service while sharing my story and hopefully help someone and perhaps myself, then we've all won. I will not shy away from describing the feelings I was having, or the difficulties I was experiencing. One of the goals of this book is to help you, the reader, find peace of mind and prosperity in the second half of your life, especially if you have experienced a life-altering injury.

We producers are some of the world's best sales executives. We get an idea and then we have to "sell it" or convince a network, studio, or distributor to give us money for the project, money that is equivalent to what it takes to build an office building or an apartment building. We ask them to give us a lot of money for an idea or a concept that someone else dreamed up. It is the ultimate intangible. That takes real skill. Initially, I wondered if I would ever have a producing career again. However, as the saying goes, necessity is the mother of invention. What I can tell you is that I was betting my life savings that I would be able to recreate myself as a university lecturer as well as a motivational, inspirational speaker and an author of non-fiction books if I couldn't produce again.

Psychiatrist Scott Peck, who wrote *The Road Less Traveled,* said "Life is difficult." It was so for him, and in spite of all his medical and empirical knowledge, those closest to him said he left this planet a broken man. Apparently, he was an unrecovered alcoholic with many unresolved relationship issues. If the last thing you ever imagined was that you would be facing a health issue or financial challenges, that your business would close unexpectedly, that you would experience family, friendship, or marriage difficulties or, God forbid, the loss of a loved one, then welcome to the club. You are no longer alone.

How To Read This Book

I have been using the Eight Steps of the Master Mind Principle myself with great success for over 15 years.

The first thing I want to share with you is that this book is not a traditional self-help publication. It utilizes the Eight Steps of the Master Mind Principles to help you, the reader, overcome whatever adversity it is you are facing, and find peace of mind and prosperity. My style of writing is also more conversational than a formal behavioral science tome.

In Part One, you will be taken on a road trip down memory lane to another time. It will be part biographical and part philosophical. It is important for you, the reader, to know my experience.

Part Two utilizes my daily journal as the framework, to allow the events to unfold as they were happening to me, in real time. This process began the first week of July 2013 and ended where I am today, August 15, 2016, I have done a major rewrite in light of the events that have occurred since starting the book. Those journal sections will have the text inside of a box. At the same time, you will be introduced to the Eight Steps of the Master Mind Principle. I will draw upon my interdisciplinary background to explain to you how you might work these steps into all areas of your life. I will use my journey as the backbone of Part Two and to demonstrate how it is I applied the steps to overcome the difficulties I was facing and continue to face.

What I can say today with certainty is that the circumstances of my life have already changed for the better as a result of employing these steps. If you just want help or are in a crisis, then please feel free to proceed immediately to Part Two.

Part One

Chapter One

Let Me Introduce Myself

On the next page is a picture of me in Toronto in the summer of 1964. I was 16 years old. I want to let you know where I came from and what I've learned during my lifetime. This will give you a sense of who I am today, and why you might be interested in what I have to say. If I were you, I would certainly want to know, Who is this man and why should I pay any attention to him? Although I have outlined some of my past successes in the foreword, you may still be asking just what qualifies me to write a self-help book? After all, you may be a captain of industry, a lawyer, physician, engineer, housewife, banker, politician, or an everyday working woman or man.

To answer the above-mentioned questions, let us go back and start in the 1960s. If you can remember the 1960s, then you weren't there, according to my friends. What does this mean? To start with, we shared the live hard, die young and leave a good-looking corpse philosophy, based on ignorance of facts and inaccurate data. I was so naïve at that age. In truth, I had a very privileged background.

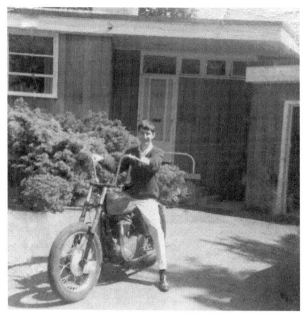

At 16, I was a rebel, and I drove a motorcycle. Was I dangerous? Not in my private-school blazer, or my button-down white shirt, or my Bass Weejuns penny loafers. I rode a BSA 650 motorcycle, and I loved the speed and freedom it gave me. And I was the first young man at my private school that drove one. It had straight pipes, no front fender, and the license plate was sitting off the back lock nut, holding the wheel on. It looked cool.

As I look back at that photograph today, I just smile. But here is what I was like. I would start drinking with a small group of my like-minded friends. I would end up on that motorcycle in Toronto, where I lived. Most of my friends grew up in Rosedale or Moore Park in Toronto. My mother and I were in Deer Park, the area just north of St. Clair that ran between Yonge Street on the east and Avenue Road on the west. These were nice neighborhoods. I would arrive at a young lady's house, park the BSA out front and stroll up to the door feeling like Peter

Fonda on steroids.

Now, when I wasn't drinking, I was so shy it was hard to get a word out of me. But, after imbibing a few, my mind said that I could give Don Juan a run for his money. On a few occasions, the mothers would say, "David, my daughter is not going out with you on that machine!" I'd lean up against the door just like I'd seen Jean-Paul Belmondo do in the French New Wave cinema that was the rage at the time and say, "What are you doing? Want to come for a ride?" They didn't all slam the door in my face. I was bad. But it was fun. At least a few times, I was very pleasantly surprised. Hello, Mrs. Robinson.

Honest to God, as I think of it now, and being a parent with four of my own kids (including two daughters) and four grandkids, I just think back on those days, shake my head and smile. I was so innocent. I also say a prayer:

"Please forgive me for all the crazy things I did, but never please let me forget how enjoyable it was." I want to state for the record that I was a disaster as a student back then. I always quit high school near the end of the year so I wouldn't fail. I never opened a book, except once. I was at a private cram school, Meisterschaft College, right behind my former prep school, De La Salle Oakland, on Woodlawn Avenue.

To the best of my memory, I was writing a Grade 12 geography exam. The night before I thought, "I'd better at least look at the textbook." My poor mother was paying several thousand dollars a year in 1967 for me to attend this private school for teenagers like me who had a lot of "learning issues." Like never showing up. I would get drunk most days after lunch at the Embassy Tavern or the Place Pigalle on Avenue Road. Then I would be obnoxious to the teachers. To the outside world, we appeared rich and spoiled (which in my case was not the reality since my mom made an astounding sacrifice for me to attend). That said, the teachers were actually very good.

I found the book interesting and stayed up reading it. It had my attention. The other only subject I had enjoyed this much had been British history. Canadian history bored me to death.

The next morning I wrote the exam and the following day, the teacher, Jay, asked me to stay after school. When I arrived, he sat me down. "Whom did you cheat from?" he asked. I looked at him and said, "What are you talking about?" He smiled oddly, as if he'd caught me dead in my tracks. "You have the highest mark in the class. I know you've never even come close to a mark like this before." I smiled right back at him and with real confidence said, "I read the book."

I can still remember the look on his face of total disbelief. "Oh yeah, would you sit here right now and write it again?" As best as I can remember, I smiled and said, "Sure, but if I ace it I want to drive your Corvette." He had the sweetest 1964 (or 65) green Stingray.

He said something like, "You bet." I sat down and rewrote the exam and scored even higher. He was very surprised by those results. That started a friendship with this teacher where he and I would go out drinking after school, and I would tell him about our Rock & Roll business, which stunned him even more. He couldn't believe what my friend John Brower and I were doing. And he lent me the Corvette.

My Early Career

At this time, my brother Jim got me a job on the floor of the Toronto Stock Exchange. It was there that I would get my fundamental lesson in economics. My first position was as a post boy. As a post boy, I would mark the various stock prices that were being bid and the various brokers would yell at me to change the prices. Then I worked as a phone clerk for a brokerage firm. During this same period, my oldest friend, John Brower, who much later appeared in my studio's production of *Yonge Street, Toronto Rock & Roll Stories*, began talking about our getting serious about starting up a record company.

In the summer of 1967, John Brower, Bob McBride, who would go on to sing with the band Lighthouse (*Sunny Days, One Fine Morning*) and I boarded an American Airlines flight to Los Angeles. That was the beginning of the career that I've carried on with to this day, with stops along the way to educate myself.

During that summer in Los Angeles, my life changed totally. It was as a result of that experience, and then coming back to Toronto, that I realized I couldn't safely drink alcohol. In March 1970, at the age of 22, I stopped drinking. I have never had another drink to this day, 46 years later.

At 21, I found myself working full time on the floor of the Toronto Stock Exchange at a Montreal brokerage firm, Bouchard and Company. Once again, through my brother Jim, I would meet my second oldest best friend that I still have today, Mike O'Shea, who was my immediate supervisor. Those were the days when I'd go out for lunch, have about six quick drinks in a row, and then go back and start taking orders from Mike for the Pro Trader, Bobby Dunbar. Somehow, though, I always managed to pull it off.

Also at the age of 21, I was married for the first time. That marriage only lasted a few years. It was at this time that I utilized my experience of working in the brokerage business and went to work as a financial planner. I spent three years with two major Canadian insurance companies before my manager and I formed ASK

Corporation. We sought out the advice of Bob Proctor, who was early in his career in the human potential movement. Through him and my manager, we ended up purchasing one of the Earl Nightingale Distributorships, which allowed us to get into the business of motivating and inspiring both individuals and corporations through Earl's audio programs. It was through this experience that I acquired my early experience in public speaking.

I'm grateful to say that my first marriage produced my two oldest children, Andrew and Colleen. They are both married today and have children of their own, and it's been a wonderful experience reconnecting with them. Andrew had the opportunity to work with me when he came out of university. My ex-wife Bev and I now drive together to see our daughter Colleen and to visit her, her husband Rob, and two of my grandkids, Guerin and Conlan. They live in Franklin, near

Nashville Tennessee. I am so proud of all my kids.

Higher Education

When my first marriage ended, I made the decision to return to school and went to Humber College in Toronto to study journalism. I'd always wanted to be a writer.

After two years, I transferred to Simon Fraser University (SFU) in Burnaby, British Columbia. That is the only decision I've ever made that I've regretted as it took me out of Andrew's and Colleen's lives for almost 15 years, except for the occasional visit. I was studying communications — not film and television — which include behavioral sciences and Gregory Bateson's Systems Theory. I was working toward becoming an alcohol and drug counselor.

My Introduction to Filmmaking

After my undergraduate studies, I was admitted to graduate school at SFU. It was there that I made my first film, *Alcohol, Drugs and the Young in British Columbia*, with the Royal Canadian Mounted Police in North Vancouver.

I received an A for that film. That made me think, "Hmm, sit in an office and listen to people go on about life, or travel around the world, meet interesting people and have a whole lot of fun making films." It took about a nanosecond to make that choice.

During this time, I also began my first teaching assignment working as a teaching assistant for the chair of the department, Bill Melody, and his long-time friend and associate, Dallas Smythe. They were both political economists.

After I had made the decision to stop studying the behavioral sciences, I met and began producing movies with my late business partner, Phillip Borsos. Those years were remarkable and out of them would come tremendous critical success. In 1980, I accompanied Phillip to the Academy Awards as a result of his nomination for *Nails*. By now I owned 40% of Phil's company and had helped finance the finishing of *Nails*.

I am grateful to say that I had an amazing life as a result of that decision. Less than two years later we would be launched onto the world stage with *The Grey Fox*, which was nominated for two Golden Globe Awards, Best Foreign Picture, and Best Actor, Richard Farnsworth. Francis Ford Coppola's Zoetrope Studios presented the film, and United Artists Classics distributed it. In between those two projects

It was an amazing experience the morning it was announced that *The Grey Fox* had been nominated for two Golden Globe Awards. It is also the only film that Roger Ebert ever reviewed twice.

We would end up winning seven Genies that same year (Canadian Academy Awards) and be recognized by the international press for producing what would become one of the most critically acclaimed movies in the history of Canada. The 22nd Government of Canada made a commemorative stamp of it.

Next I was executive producer on a small feature, *Till Death Do Us Part*, which received very positive reviews in the U.S. trade papers and the Canadian press.

Those were heady years.

Crash and Burn

About two years later, I would experience the first major reversal of my life on a feature film I was producing in Washington State. We had paid $25,000 for financing to a law firm in New York City. The lawyers said they had $4 million on deposit, and they would advance the funds once we paid the above-mentioned standby fee. We paid their fee and the funds never materialized. We were the victims of commercial fraud. I would end up owing over $5 million dollars Canadian, most of which has now been repaid. I did not go bankrupt because I felt I would never learn what I needed to learn if I did that. That experience propelled me to finally get honest with myself and to take 100% responsibility for the fact that I had made the decision to move ahead with a project that would have been better off being left alone.

Once again, this would end up being the greatest learning experience I had ever had, and my life changed for the better. Mind you, I couldn't see it at that moment. All I could see was the mountain of debt and the number of people we'd hurt.

The reason I added the "second half of life" to the subtitle of this book is because it was that experience, which took place when I was at the threshold of middle age and the beginning of the second half of my life, that would propel me toward the most productive, peace-filled and, yet ironically, challenging times I ever had. Back then I was working toward re-establishing my career. My wife and I were raising two young children and acquiring a nice home back in Deer Park, the same Toronto neighborhood I'd grown up in. We were educating our youngest children, and I was re-establishing my relationship with my two older children from my first marriage, who were now young adults.

My Introduction to Pedagogy

It was during this period that I began my teaching career. My first faculty position was at York University in Toronto. After four or five years, I moved to Ryerson University in downtown Toronto. What I learned at those two institutions is that I had a real gift for teaching and communicating. Ironically, if I hadn't had the problems on the previously mentioned production, I would never have undertaken either one of those positions. What a wonderful gift teaching is, and I hope to do it again.

While teaching, I founded three production companies, each of which ended up being very successful.

In the past 28 years I have written, produced, or directed over 130 episodes of primetime television along with four feature films. There has been a significant list of awards we've either been nominated for or have won. Generally, my life has been remarkable, in spite of the occasional speed bump brought on by indecision, impatience, self-centeredness, anger, or fear — fear that I would not get what I wanted or lose what I had. It has been filled with so many wonderful events and people that I just sit here amazed at where I've been and the people I've met. While I do have a few regrets, they are not many. What I have is a rich treasure trove of memories and accomplishments and an outstanding cadre of family, friends, and associates with whom I've spent my entire life.

Chapter Two

My Generation

"People try to put us d-down (Talkin' 'bout my generation)" — The Who

If you were born between 1945 and 1965 you will remember the refrain, "Don't trust anyone over 30." We were the generation that created that myth, and we are the generation that can change it. Conversely, if we were operating out of the flawed paradigm of that day and applying it to our lives today, we'd say, "Don't trust anyone under 50." I really believe now that nothing could be further from the truth.

Today's younger generation is so much more responsible than ours was. I'd like to be like them when I grow up.

The bill of goods we sold ourselves about youth being the only way, the better way, the enlightened way, that being groovy and hip was the best, was flawed. However, many of the principles of our youth were sound. Make love, not war (just not to so many people ... it's not good for you or anyone else that matter). Social justice, right on. Reconciling with our First Nations citizens is vital to the health of our country.

My Take on Neurobiology

Finding an answer to war — what do we need to do to realize we are operating out of a part of our brain that is millions of years old and that relying on our brain will never work? Violence will never solve any problems, and yet it is often the first avenue that we pursue. Violence is hard-wired into our brains. Our reptilian/mammalian brain is connected that way to save us from aggressive predators. The only trouble is that there are no more dinosaurs on the planet. But you can't tell that to our brainstem. According to

Dr. Paul MacLean, the triune brainstem is responsible for aggression, territorial and reproductive behavior. These behaviors are the primary triggers for all of our problems in life.

While the triune brainstem was helpful for our survival, hundreds of thousands, or even millions of years ago, it ends up causing us untold grief, regret, and pain when we let it control our body and minds. It will have us say and do things that, when we are not in our "right mind," we should never say or do. Essentially we have outdated the software in our brains. That is why we need to utilize tools like the Eight Steps, to reprogram our thinking so we can overcome these ancient triggers that create so many problems for us.

My Take on Sociology

Society's worshipping at the altar of youth has ended up creating a massive schism that is both counter-intuitive and counter-productive.

Ironically, what some advertisers thought was a dream come true in the 18- to 35-year-old demographic has proven to be less than perfect. As it turns out, according to some economists, it is our aging population, including the baby boomers, that is controlling the purse strings of the world's economy and we are in charge of over 80% of wealth on the planet today. We still have a voracious appetite for spending and consuming, on either quality projects like philanthropy, art, and culture, or on consumer goods. Boomers just love cars, motorcycles, motor homes, vacation homes, travel, food, alcohol, and gifts for those we love. But are the latter the only things we should be pursuing? If we believe they are the key to our happiness, it might be a good idea if those beliefs are analyzed one more time.

How happy are you with your Mercedes Benz, BMW, or Lexus, a beach house in California, a condo in Florida, or a home in the

Hamptons? There is nothing wrong with any of those items if you are also using your resources to make a difference in the world. I have a Mercedes myself.

EGO
(Edge God Out)

However, if all you are doing is satisfying an insatiable urge to have more in order to appease your ego, then watch out, as you may not really be a happy camper. The question you might want to ask yourself is, What have you done lately to make a difference on the planet if you are fortunate enough to be in a position to help others?

I recently had lunch with a woman, Pamela Bendall, who is a boomer and who, in her previous life, was a very successful stockbroker. She had just published her book, *What Was I Thinking?* It is a must read. In it she describes fulfilling her dream of building her own 47-foot sailboat, *Precious Metal*, and sailing singlehanded from British Columbia down to the South Pacific in 2008. That took incredible skill, courage, and a sense of self that most people will never find. Did she just sail for her gratification? No, and as a result of her travels, she has started up schools in Mexico and is now educating over 7,000 children. The UN decided to make her organization an example of what an individual can do during the Year of Education.

Have you, like me, found that those material pursuits alone are very short-lived one-way love affairs? That they only supply us with a very temporary sense of satisfaction and little or no peace of mind? I have. I remember getting the new Chrysler 300 the year after it was rereleased in 2006. I wasn't off the lot and down the street a few miles when my mind started up. "Why didn't I get the 300 C," I asked myself? "I like that metallic gray one. Why did I get a black one?"

What about those of us who haven't planned for our futures as well as we should have? What will happen to us? Once again my mind starts up. "You will end up penniless, a pauper working a corner with a cup!"

If we keep our wits about us, this need not happen. Youth is fine for backbreaking and heavy slugging, but the intellect of those who are more mature, gifted with our wealth of experience, is worth its weight in gold. And we can all realize this with some simple steps and planning. If you can remember back when life was "groovy," you'll remember that we didn't have a care in the world. That is a great place to get back to. And it's attainable. How? By simply following the recipe, laid out in Part Two of this book, and the later chapters with the Eight Steps of the Master Mind. Did we have a lot of money? No, probably not. But we likely had friends and fun.

What's the truth about being young? Our bodies are supple. We have higher sex drives. We can take falls and brushes with death more easily. Physically, we have more energy. We have great expectations. We have wonderful plans. We have a lot of living to look forward to. And we think we are immortal.

The Truth About Being a Baby Boomer and Aging

What is the truth about being a "baby boomer," being a Sage? Many of us still have a good sex drive. It is, however, much more emotional and psychological than physical. In many cases, it is based on true intimacy rather than raw, self-centered sexual satisfaction.

We do our best to avoid falls and brushes with death through an acquired wisdom and expericnce. We can still have wonderful expectations, and we can head out and try novel things with a new confidence — our lives won't end if we fail. We can still ski, ride motorcycles and bikes, take hikes, travel, and go on road trips and visit places we've always wanted to.

We can try new adventures or new occupations where we don't have to feel shame or blame if we don't bat a thousand. There is a wonderful book by Paul Kurtz entitled *The Spirituality of Imperfection.* In it, Kurtz points out that, in baseball, if you hit 300, you will be paid millions of dollars to join a major league baseball team. What that means is that 7 out of 10 times you will miss hitting the ball. Baseball is the only game in the world that recognizes errors as part of the process. We want to liberate ourselves from old beliefs, old self-defeating thinking that we acquired somewhere between the ages of 3 and 12. None of us are perfect, and every one of us makes mistakes — and that includes you and me!

So many of us have unresolved issues from our pasts and our childhoods. It is imperative that we let go of old, self-defeating thinking about our dreams or ideas that we had in our youth that no longer support us. It is important to age gracefully.

Holding onto the idea that we need to be liked by everyone is self-defeating. Not everyone will like us. As a matter of fact, what others think of us is none of our business. It's more important to like ourselves, just the way we are and not worry about what others think of us, period. In the majority of cases, anyone over 50 has a tad of flab. Can we look at ourselves in the mirror and say, "I love you just as you are, balding, chubby, and wrinkled?" If not, here is an area that we need to examine.

Do I have complete freedom from this? I do not. I still glance sideways in the mirror, hold in my stomach and puff up my chest. Once again, there is that old reptilian brainstem firing up. Today, I try to thank my brainstem and mind for sharing and then give them permission to take the day off.

Our youthful years were a wonderful time. So is aging. It is one of the great treasures that many of us do not get to enjoy. Is it filled with challenges? Yes. Our loved ones get sick and die. Our friends move away. Other friends change and go from outgoing positive people to reclusive, angry, and lonely folks that slowly withdraw from life. All we can do is wish them well and bless them. We do get lonely. We do sometimes think, "What's the point of all this?"

For many of us, it is often hard to accept that not only are we getting older, but also we are now in our "mature" years. There's that word again. Mature. There are some of us who've had unhappy childhoods; unfortunately, they've lasted 50 or 60 years. The good news is that it's never too late to have a happy childhood!

I don't know about you, but I don't feel old.

I can still do everything I did at 20, or 30, or 40. I can ski, swim (which I try and do at least twice a week), and I can hike up the side of mountains in Northern California along rugged logging roads. I have to stop occasionally, but so do 40-year-olds. I can still dance (I don't know about the Watusi). I can still make love without needing a little pill (although I just tried one, and they're fabulous).

However, we are mature (hopefully) adults who should strive to be role models of how it is to age gracefully and with purpose. To try and act like a teenager, or dress in the current style of young adults is playing a form of emotional and psychological Russian roulette.

When we realize that we no longer have the body we had at 25, 35, 45, or 55, I don't think it's a good idea for us to take hormone replacement or take up some extreme form of exercise to try and emulate someone half our age. My gut instinct is it is a tragedy waiting to happen. If it is something prescribed by a physician for health reasons, that is a different story. I was stunned to find out that the medical license I paid 50 bucks for online wasn't valid. So, I'm out of the medical advice dispensing business.

I am not talking about physical fitness either. We all should pursue that. In addition to my swimming, I try to do aqua fit classes at least two days a week, but three is optimal. I also do 50 push-ups off the side of my bathtub three mornings a week. I walk everywhere I can. I make a point of leaving my car at home if I can. So exercise is good. Trying to emulate Generation Y? Not so much.

Having the self-confidence to be able to dress however we want is healthy. If we're doing it to please ourselves and just have fun, fabulous. But if were desperately doing it to cling on to the illusion of youth, well, that can be embarrassing. Our job is to be happy where we are at this stage of our lives. I still love my button-down shirts and penny loafers. I just wish I could fit into my school blazer!

Faith?

Faith. For many of us it is critical to our well-being. Again, I want to emphasize, I'm not necessarily talking about religion, although if you have a traditional faith that works for you, then you are ahead of the game. Our focus is on a faith in something greater than we are. It doesn't matter if it's your local hydro provider.

I've been an agnostic a lot of my life. I had great faith when I was young, and then as I studied and educated myself beyond my level of comprehension, I lost my childhood faith. It didn't make sense to me in light of scientific and empirical evidence (or so I thought).

Here is how my brain functions and how my "faulty filter" kicks in (stay tuned for an explanation). Look at the randomness of the planet. Who can understand why such natural disasters as the horrific earthquake and the Indian Ocean tsunami that killed over 240,000 people in 13 countries on December 26, 2004 needed to happen if there is a loving Supreme Being? Then there is the insanity of the shootings at Sandy Hook Elementary School that happened on December 14, 2012. What about the fact that the Nazis killed 6 million Jews and others during the Second World War in concentration camps?

Joseph Stalin killed close to 30 million of his citizens. I'm sure they all believed in God and prayed for help. But where was God in these times? It makes me wonder, and my wonder was portrayed in the wonderful Hollywood film that many critics consider the best film of all time — *Casablanca* — when Humphrey Bogart's Rick says to Ingrid Bergman's Ilsa, "I've got a job to do, too. Where I'm going, you can't follow. What I've got to do, you can't be any part of, Ilsa. I'm no good at being noble, but it doesn't take much to see that the problems of three little people don't amount to a hill of beans in this crazy world. Someday you'll understand that."

It is true that our problems won't amount to a hill of beans, except to us. Who can remember what they were worried about 10 years ago, five years ago, six months ago? I can guarantee you, though, at the time you thought it was such a crisis you never thought you would find a solution.

As a result of those horrible circumstances, you may have thought that your life was over. But now you can hardly remember what it was that was so bad. We have to exclude experiencing the death of a loved one, being seriously ill, being cheated on by a partner, or losing a business from this situation. Those hurts cut deep and to the bone and take both time and psychological or spiritual assistance to heal. So how do we reconcile a Divine Being who allows these horrific events to transpire with someone who is filled with love for all humanity? Rabbi Harold Kushner in his groundbreaking book, *When Bad Things Happen to Good People*, does a much better job of explaining it than I can.

These unexplained horrific events are some of the great paradoxical mysteries of life. And one I don't think we will get a real answer to anytime soon. It is only when we shuffle off this mortal coil and then find ourselves either in a very deep slumber for all eternity, or, present in the radiance of a Supreme Being whom I'm willing to bet will not be standing there with a clipboard, a scowl on His/Her/Its face, and saying either verbally or telepathically, "Hi Dave, I've been expecting you." Then, a large trap door opens and I find myself being hurled into the endless pit of fire.

Alas, that's how my childhood mind works.

Talk about insanity. And that's after the Catholic Church canceled Hell as a geographic location a few decades ago. But it is so deeply ingrained in my unconscious that it is the first place my mind goes whenever I find myself in my normal state of being a human being who makes mistakes.

What kind of God would create a species, then fry their derrière off for being exactly the way they were made; imperfect in every way. Flawed emotions, flawed values, flawed instincts that run wild (lust, jealousy, rage, greed), and flawed physiology that wears out and dies.

Or, is it that there is a rhythm to life that always ends in a transformative stage at death? (Or, at least what we call death.) What if it is simply a gateway to another reality, another dimension that is parallel to this one?

Today there are a growing number of quantum physicists who believe this is the case, and they estimate they are only a decade or two away from discovering its mystery. What is the common thread here? It is all the information that is coming into my brain and being processed by my limbic system — and it is part of the old brainstem. So, while the brain has added new hemispheres in the neo-cortex and the temporal lobes that actually are responsible for our wondering about God, it's the old reptilian guy/gal up there who is running the show. Time to let him/her go.

Acceptance

A very wise man, who was a doctor and an alcoholic once said (and I paraphrase), "Acceptance is the key to all of our problems in life." When we rail against time, the fact we have aged, when we rail against the injustices of the monetary system, the (supposed) free markets that we embrace, the people whom we perceive have harmed us, the government, our ex-husbands or wives, we cannot find peace of mind or happiness. Whatever it is we are not happy with, it is our problem, not the other person's. We don't accept injustice either. But we need to be prudent in how we find a solution. We don't get out of our automobiles and confront an erratic driver who may be impaired and dangerous. We call 911 in North America, or whatever the number is in the country in which you are reading this, and we let our law enforcement agencies handle the situation. Trying to take the law into our hands is actually dangerous and can lead to tragic events, as was witnessed with the horrible murder of the young Trayvon Martin in Florida in 2012.

When it comes to families, many of us have had situations where family members had difficulty communicating appropriately because of anger or fear. They say and do things that are not acceptable. Many of us have had to seek outside help to overcome the challenges of living in a dysfunctional family situation created by alcohol, drugs, anger, or abandonment. It is important to remember that many of these people who hurt us might be suffering from a disease. So, acceptance of their condition is important, but it is also never appropriate to accept their behavior when they are being abusive

Chapter Three

Time Flies When You Are Having Fun!

So, there I was, minding my own business at age 39, in a second marriage with two young children. I had just lost a lot of money on a movie I was producing, and I calculated I had a good 25 to 30 years to make a comeback. No problem. Relaxed, I went to bed and woke up at age 65. I was stunned. How could this be? I wish I'd planned better. But the time between 39 and 65 flew by like a rocket. You might say that it was like riding the head of a ballistic missile, unguided, as it would turn out. When I stopped and tooj stock, here is where I was. I have a nice home in the country, mostly paid for, and a nice apartment in Toronto. I had a reasonable amount of savings.

As a producer what I had was the talent and ability to conceive an idea and translate that onto the screen so that significant numbers of people would want to watch what we created and produced. More importantly, in the past, when I made 10 pitches, I would end up with between three and five productions on average. More recently, though, I went through 335 nos. Obviously, I was not connecting on any of these projects.

My last four productions had started before I was assaulted and injured, except for one, which my brother Jim gave me. That was the "Super Volcano, Yellowstone's Fury" production. My youngest son, Brendan, and Anthony Wallace, who works with me, came up with our two previous Vision Productions. We sat on pins and needles in 2013 waiting for word, but none came.

What were my choices? I decided to focus on a new career of writing and speaking. I would see if I could be hired again to a teaching position. I'd like to. I had won a teaching award, so I knew I have that ability. I knew I would need to make a decision. And so will you! Especially if you are about to embark on any major changes in your life due to a financial setback, the loss of a job or management position. Or, if you are one of the boomers who are fortunate enough to be retiring, you might have been affected by the financial meltdown that occurred after 2008. You might have experienced the loss of your spouse or life partner or your closest friends. You might have recently been diagnosed with a life-altering illness, whether it's terminal or not. It's important for any of us, whether we are self-employed or work as an executive or manager or as a frontline employee, to do an inventory of our assets.

That inventory should include not only our financial assets, but also our family, friends, health, mementos of our past, keepsakes from our children, awards, and a list of our achievements. It is a very good idea to do this. It is also important to sit down and look at every aspect of your finances too.

Why? Because the same brain that lies to us will also try to convince us that we are completely deficient. My mind often tells me, "I don't have all the skills necessary to proceed with something that is out of my comfort zone." It might say, "You've worked at Acme Tool and Gear all of your life, and now you want to start up a bookstore cafe. How crazy is that?" Not very if you are innovative and add things like coffee, comfortable chairs, author's readings, a gift shop, book club and make it a center for the community. Earlier in this process I signed up with Jack Canfield Coaching because I couldn't close deals. I am committed to healing myself and moving forward, and I am trying to do everything within my power to mitigate the situation of having lost that ability.

And while the coaching may not solve that

specific problem, it has already brought to light this very point. I have had a lot of success in my life, which my brain can conveniently forget, and thus my mind tells me "loser." Once again, I must say to my mind, "Thank you for sharing and you can have the rest of the day off."

Here is what is ironic about my occupation. I was yelled at as a child in school for daydreaming. Here I am a lifetime later, and I've been paid enormously well to sit around and dream up ideas. Again, as I said, my body of work is fairly extensive. Here's the thing. As a writer and producer I get an idea, and I go and sit in meetings with executives at studios or networks and say, "Here we go." And off I go explaining a concept. Then, on average, 3 out of 10 times (batting 300) they say, "Okay, we like it." And then we sit down and negotiate for months on end, and finally the day comes when a contract arrives, all based on an idea that we've created.

That is a rare gift, a real creative gift that I had. However, as I said, I've hit a wall. In 2013, we finished four productions, including an award-winning series. Then, it all just came to an abrupt end after the physical assault.

But, instead of giving up and admitting defeat, I stayed committed to moving forward by taking an inventory of my skills. I am creative, and I am a good communicator. I love people and people tend to like me. I want to be of service because I can help others who have experienced similar hardships to what I have experienced over the past few years. The good news for all of us is that there is plenty of help if you want it. You just have to look for it. You Are Not Alone

Each of our stories is different. Yet our stories may share many similarities. There are those whose lives are altered because of a serious car accident or industrial accident. Or they may have experienced the loss of their marriage, the death of a partner. Perhaps someone close to you is suffering from the family disease of alcoholism or drug addiction. Others of us may be having difficulties with our children or challenges with our siblings, or recovering from the financial meltdown that has been plaguing us.

Here is the good news. If I can find a way out, so can you. And here is the key: you are not to blame. You may have to take responsibility for what's happened to you and not get caught up in a victim stance, but you don't have to give up.

We may also have to change course in life. For any of you who are sailors, you know that frequently we have to tack when we're heading into the wind and go in the opposite direction to get to where we are going. At times, it will appear we are going the wrong way as we go to a starboard tack to a port tack. And we may have to be ready to let go of old ideas in the event that there is something new trying to make its way into our life.

There are countless millions of others out there going through the same thing that you and I are. The key is to find fellow travelers with whom you can share your journey in a safe environment and thus overcome whatever adversity life throws at you.

We deserve to enjoy the benefits of our hard work in these "golden years" in a way our parents or grandparents could never have ever imagined. "We are the champions," as Freddy Mercury sang in his iconic hit song with his band Queen back in the 70s.

So, how you ended up here was by showing up and not dying. From the point at age 35 until today seems like it's only been a few years. It's over 30! To many people, it's half a lifetime. It's gone by so quickly. So, what I have accomplished?

Taking Stock of Our Lives

The one thing that Jack Canfield's coaching did was make me aware of a very important fact. One of our exercises was to create an inventory of my successes. And I have had many more successes than failures. But at that time, my mind was saying, "All you've done is fail." I don't know about you, but my mind lies to me. The old "faulty filter"!

So, what is the truth? Yes, we've had disappointments. Who hasn't? But as a result of taking responsibility for them and doing the work that needed to be done, I've been able to clean up the wreckage of my past. Financially I've probably paid back 80% or 90% of the people I harmed through indebtedness. And, more importantly, I've never had any of those kinds of financial problems again. And even though I am facing difficulty today, my banks know exactly where I am and what my plans are. I'm not hiding from anyone.

I was married a second time to a very funny lady, Deborah. As a result of that union, we have two children who are now young adults, Brendan and Laurel. They have both worked with me in the past. I've already mentioned my two oldest children, Andrew and Colleen, and my four grandkids, Sophie, Guerin, Henry, and Conlan.

What else have I been able to do? When I originally wrote this book I said I was able to teach as a faculty member of two universities, York University and Ryerson University in Toronto, where I was the recipient of the CESAR teaching award. I've now added one more university, which will come along later in the book.

In addition to my film and television productions, I've been president of several film and television production companies that have enjoyed tremendous critical and financial success. I have also had the privilege of working with a lot of people over the years in a number of disciplines, and I've had the pleasure of meeting some of the most intelligent, noteworthy, and influential people on the planet. So, there is hope for you and for me. Hope that we can rebuild our lives and enjoy more of it!.

Part Two

Chapter Four

There Is a Solution

And the solution is the Eight Steps of Master Mind Principles. I've outlined my own life succinctly (I hope) and, just so you know, I'm there with you too. I'm not making this up. What are the Eight Steps created by Jack Boland?

Eight Steps Into the Master Mind Principles

1.   I SURRENDER

I admit that, of myself, I am powerless to solve my problems, powerless to improve my life. I need help.

2.   I BELIEVE

I now come to believe that a power greater than myself — The Infinite Creative Intelligence — the Master Mind can change my life.

3. I AM READY TO BE CHANGED

I realize that erroneous self-defeating thinking is the cause of my problems, unhappiness, fears and failures. I am ready to be changed so my life can be transformed.

4. I DECIDE TO BE CHANGED

I make a decision to surrender my will and my life to the Master Mind. I ask to be changed at depth.

5. I FORGIVE

I forgive myself for all my mistakes and shortcomings. I also forgive all other persons who may have harmed me.

6. I ASK

I make known my specific requests, asking my partner's support in knowing that the Master Mind is fulfilling my needs. (Make your request now: "I request ____.")

GROUP RESPONSE: "I know the Master Mind has heard you and is providing you with what you have asked for."

7.   I GIVE THANKS

I give thanks that the Master Mind is responding to my needs and I assume the same feelings I would have if my requests were fulfilled.

8.   I DEDICATE MY LIFE

I now have a covenant in which it is agreed that the Master Mind is supplying me with an abundance of all things necessary to live a successful and happy life.

I dedicate myself to be of maximum service to God and those around me, to live in a manner that sets the highest example for others to follow, and to remain responsive to God's direction.

I go forth with a spirit of enthusiasm, excitement, and expectancy. I am at peace

Adapted from Jack Boland's work at Renaissance Unity. Copyright 2005.

Setting Up a Master Mind Group

How does this work? First and foremost, check online sites that will allow all readers to hook up with other likeminded folks so you will not be alone. I'd recommend that a group be set up at your church, synagogue, temple, or fellowship or service club. It doesn't matter what religion you are, or, if you don't even have a religion.

This is God, as you understand God to be. God can be an acronym for Good Orderly Direction. It is suggested that you have no more than 4 to 6 people in your group. Everyone needs the opportunity to share and be prayed for. For many people, the idea of having their wishes affirmed is totally foreign and really uncomfortable as it takes a level of trust that many people have never experienced. There are ways around this.

If you don't belong to a church, synagogue, temple, or fellowship and you are living alone or in a retirement residence, you can go online and look up information on how to form a group. As I indicated earlier, the original principles of the Master Mind were created by Napoleon Hill early in the twentieth century if you want to Google it. Regardless of their age, the principles are as true today as they were when he revolutionized the business world by creating a new paradigm for success. In fact, Napoleon Hill is the forerunner of all the people today such as Jack Canfield, Dr. Deepak Chopra, and the late Dr. Wayne Dyer who write inspirational material, to name just a few. His insights and wisdom are timeless.

How do the steps work? I know from experience that they've worked wonders in my life. But today, the circumstances of my life are completely changed. It is my intention to be as forthright and open as I can. I want to share my journey of implementing the Eight Steps as I pursue a spiritual, emotional, as well as financial solution to my problems that will create real peace of mind.

Unity Churches across North America do have established Master Mind groups and you can check with them too.

Chapter Five

How To Work The Steps

STEP 1. I SURRENDER

I admit that, of myself, I am powerless to solve my problems, powerless to improve my life. I need help.

Are these steps the only way to solve your problems? Absolutely not! In some cases, you may need to seek professional help from financial advisors, insurance companies, banks, doctors lawyers, accountants, social workers, therapists, psychologists, psychiatrists, and other health care practitioners. I'm not suggesting for one moment we will have all the answers in these steps.

However, you can be sure that your life will improve if you practice these steps to the best of your ability. It will be helpful if you find a way to connect to a Master Mind group of your own. Either in person or online if you are living remotely or are unable to get out and have access to the Internet.

Here is what I wrote in my journal the first week of July 2013:

Toronto, July 2013

I'm really at a loss to understand how it is that after all these years of recovery, all the work I've done, all the praying and meditating, that I'm on the verge of losing a great deal of what I've worked for — my company, my home, my financial security.

We've now been turned down on 280+ submissions to broadcasters in Canada, the USA, and the UK. I've now dug into my own pocket for over a year to pay my company expenses, the rent on the apartment in Toronto and to cover all my credit cards and lines of credit.

I've put my house up for sale. I don't know what else to do, God. I've prayed and asked you consistently for over a year to help me know your will. I've prayed and sought to do your will. I've paid $5,000 to Jack Canfield Coaching. While it did not produce the results I wanted, it did help.

I've written out my goals. I've submitted so many projects, and I've asked everyone I know to help me get business.

What can I do? What should I do? One of the books I'm reading says I can ask for help and trust in you. I've tried to do that from the bottom of my heart. I've tried to turn my will and life over to your care. How do I totally let go and trust? I want to do it. I am powerless and I need help.

I don't understand how you function. I don't know where there is justice — is that the right word, or fairness, or outcomes. All I know God is I would like to let go and accept that I am

powerless and trust that I will totally be taken
care of. Help me to trust, please.

Have you ever found yourself in a situation where you just don't know what to do? Have you ever felt that life was not worth living? Maybe you've thought, the time has passed me by, and now I'm worthless, or worse yet, a burden on my family, or society because of my age?

Do you think about ending your life because the future looks hopeless, and you cannot find a solution or see a way out? Are you so filled with fear and anxiety that you cannot find any semblance of peace or purpose in your life? Are you filled with rage and resentment because of someone or some institution that you feel has hurt you? Do you feel that the whole bill of goods we were sold in our younger years is a complete fallacy and a misrepresentation of the truth? No matter how much stuff you purchase, no matter how nice your home is, no matter how well your family turned out, are you left with an impending sense of doom or loss? No matter what you acquire or accomplish, you can't fill the hole inside of you that keeps you awake at night?

Does someone you love have a substance abuse issue? Is someone you are close to an alcoholic or drug addict? Is one of your children or siblings suffering from an eating disorder or sexual addiction? Are any of your children teetering on the edge of financial ruin or cataclysmic loss because of their lifestyles? Are they hiding a problem with gambling, or being out of control with unsecured debts, including credit cards, lines of credit, or loans? Is your marriage or partnership on the rocks? Are you facing a life threatening illness? Are you on the verge of going bankrupt personally or corporately?

You would be shocked to find out just how common it is to be in these situations. We all have these thoughts or worries cross our mind from time to time. However, if you or your immediate family is one of the 70% who aren't totally independent or financially self-sufficient, then how do you get to enjoy some of the things that life offers if you are independently wealthy?

But there are solutions. There are many fellow travelers who have faced and overcome these feelings of being powerless over their fears and worries, as well as overcome their maladaptive self-defeating behaviors.

The key to finding a solution to any of our problems is to admit that we are powerless over these conditions, including people, places, or things, and admitting that we do need help. Once we do admit this, we can begin the process of letting go and finding real peace of mind, true happiness, and a genuine purpose in life regardless of our current circumstances. The first and most important thing that any of us must do is acknowledge there is a problem or a situation with which we need help.

Denial does not just apply to people with alcohol, drugs, mental illness, or other addictive behaviors. Accepting that we are powerless and that we need help opens the door to guidance and support from those whose lives would be enriched by assisting us. Just as your life will be when it is your turn to help a fellow traveler on the road to a better life. Who wants to admit defeat or acknowledge that we are in need of help? Pride is an awful flaw in most of us. It blinds us to our true self-worth. It keeps us locked into unhealthy self-defeating thinking and lonely lives because we don't want to look foolish, stupid, or like a failure. These are all subjective views of ourselves that are self-defeating. When we're not in a great space, we can be ruthless with ourselves. We beat ourselves up at times for making normal mistakes. We beat ourselves into feeling less than worthy and being shame-filled.

My Faulty Filter

One of my key defects is I that have a "faulty filter": I hear what isn't said, believe what isn't true, and interpret what isn't meant. I want to clarify this statement. My faulty filter applies to my thinking, not to the reality of the events in my life, or the world out there. For instance, my faulty filter wanted me to minimize what had happened to me when I was assaulted. It wanted me to dismiss those events because I didn't want anyone not to like me (codependency). If I had followed through on my initial thought not to do anything, I would have potentially caused myself, and my family, irreparable harm by listening to my faulty filter (mind).

That is why it was so good to have sober counsel from my friends and Master Mind partners who said, "You need to take care of yourself." To get my attention, my brother Jim had to scream at me so that I would do something about it.

My best friend in New York City who was my attorney also said, "You have to report this to the police because you may need medical attention and if you don't do it within a specific period, then you will impede your chance to make a claim. It has to be on record because brain injuries take time to manifest." How right he was!

My other good friend, who had also been my lawyer since 1982, said, "You have to do this. It's for your own good."

I have to tell you I felt horrible going to the police. Everyone I talked to said I had to report the attack. I felt sick inside when I went to the courts and then to a lawyer. I wanted everyone to like me, and this was such a personal situation.

I also have a faulty filter around worry. Ninety-five percent of what we worry about never comes to pass. The other 5% we bring on ourselves. Worry is praying for what you don't want. Do you know anyone who is immune from worry? There are some who claim to be. There seem to be those who really do have all the neural pathways, neurons, and serotonin receptors working properly, but it is more likely they really don't work that well.

There are Zen Masters, Spiritual Giants, and the likes of those who don't seem to worry. I wish I were one of them. I worry when I don't have anything to worry about. But that's me.

I've spent an entire lifetime trying to overcome the various elements of my life that I'm powerless over. Here is what I can say with absolute certainty: I am powerless over anything that changes my brain and thus the way I feel. So, I have to ensure that I don't consume any alcohol or drugs unless a physician prescribes them. I might also add sweets when I'm stressed out.

My mind says you can have one sugarless

ice cream cone a month in the summer. Somehow I'm reasonably okay with that one. However, that's my personality, and I'm powerless over it (truth be known, I can't have just one!). Damn I hate that. Albert Einstein said, "We can't solve problems by using the same kind of thinking we used when we created them."

We all need help from time to time, which can come from a variety of sources. There are many worthwhile self-help books, courses, and support groups. We must avail ourselves of these assets and those groups in order to find the solutions we need that will make our lives richer, more peaceful and joyful, regardless of our financial situation.

As a result of my injury, my ability to earn a living has been dramatically affected. As a result, I needed help and still need help. But here's the thing — I'm powerless over the fact that I can't seem to do what I was able to do so successfully in the past.

What were my choices? I thought I might have to give up producing. However, I'm grateful to say that I will go out on a high, creatively. I have a nice house in the country. It is an asset. I have disability insurance Which has offset some financial concerns. so I will have to see what that entails. I often revisit what my priorities are.

Mental illness is a horrible affliction. I've had my issues in my life, but never those kinds of gut-wrenching, emotional minefields that mental illness brings on.

As I said earlier, I had to quit drinking at 22, and I've never had a drink since. What I can say is that I had severe emotional issues that manifested themselves in my drinking, but my drinking was just a symptom.

Ironically, that was the reason I was there to speak to this young man — to explain how I had stopped drinking and that I'd done drugs as a young man and had been able to stop those too. In the case of this young man, it appears that his young adult onset psychosis was brought on by juvenile marijuana use.

At this stage, I had to wait and see if my injury is permanent. Furthermore, we need to wait and see whether one of the last production ideas we have is approved.

My preference would be to get back into production. To do that we've gone the extra mile in creating a wonderful "sizzle reel" (an example of what the show will look like). We sent it down in the United States to two major networks and here in Canada to another network.

I believed then from the bottom of my heart that it was going to work out. Did I manage to close these two projects or any of the others we presented? I brought in other people to help me close these deals. But ...

July 22, 2013

Real Girls of New York was turned down today. We are now down to one last idea. As a result of this news, I have to practice what I preach.

I thought that if the deals didn't come through, then hopefully my Ontario house would sell. I could use those funds to move to West Vancouver and see if I might get a faculty position at a college or university there. Without any productions going on, I would not be in a position to enjoy many of the pleasures that I would have, had my company worked out.

I was happy when I was young and without a lot of money, and I knew I could be happy again. The real joys of life are free. Most important are our relationships with our families and friends. Then our passions and hobbies, as long as they don't involve racing cars, flying planes, or taking long exotic trips to spectacular locations around the world.

There are always tapped out Tuesdays (lower movie theater ticket prices) in Canada and great deals on live theater tickets on certain days of the week. Each community we live in has municipal facilities for residents, including seniors where we can meet with people who have similar interests. I'm looking forward to that.

I also wanted to try my hand at writing a novel or two. Let's see if I can convert my idea for CANUSA Lodge into a novel. That's one idea I have had. It was a proposed television series — a bicultural comedy, which may get produced. I've also thought of converting my master's thesis into a novel, *Heaven Bound*.

And I've thought about doing seminars to go along with this book, and setting up Master Mind groups.

Shortly after all of this exciting thinking, my first ex-wife Bev called and asked me to drive to Nashville, Tennessee, with her to see our oldest daughter, her husband, and our two grandkids. It was good to get a week off and just decompress.

My Actual Road Trip to Nashville

Franklin, Tennessee

As I'm writing this, I'm sitting at my daughter and her husband's home in Franklin, Tennessee. Our drive down was really pleasant, and Bev and I were able to reconcile a lot of our old issues, letting go of the past in a very healthy and forgiving way. We were so young when we were married. Bev was a teenager. We were kids having kids.

Colleen and Rob live in a gorgeous area called Franklin. It is one of the prettiest little towns I've ever seen in my life. It is the American Dream come true.

I love Southern hospitality. One of my close friends at home in Prince Edward County, Robert, is from Memphis. My other pal Dennis and his wife Paula use to live in this area. It turns out that I have a lot of connections to Tennessee, and our great,

great, great uncle is buried here in the Civil War
Cemetery in Chattanooga.
The connections that we all have to one another
are very significant. When we begin to see just
how we are all interconnected, at some level.

In Conclusion

Acceptance of our powerlessness will also help us with our finances. If we find ourselves not having achieved our financial goals, the question we have to ask is, What do we do about it? Do we seek alternatives to money if we don't have sufficient funds to live in the lifestyle that we think we should? A unique lifestyle might include living communally or in a cooperative housing project. Can we simplify and downsize or perhaps call it "right size," as my pal Dennis says.

What we once needed to validate ourselves materially becomes less important with time. But, I think today, peace of mind is far more valuable than possessions. All the material goods in the world don't amount to the proverbial hill of beans if we are constantly in a state of fear and dread about our creditors and finances. Fearing that we will lose what we have, or that we will not get what we want, will always trigger our character flaws.

So, practically speaking, what can we do to get to a place of financial solvency and peace of mind? First, we must do a searching and fearless inventory of our emotional, spiritual, and financial lives.

Chapter Six

I Believe

STEP 2. I BELIEVE

I now come to believe that a power greater than myself — The Infinite Creative Intelligence — the Master Mind can change my life.

July 27, 2013
Well, I've just been turned down by US Cable network in New York on Real Girls of New York City. We have two options left to stay in business. The first is if a major network in LA says yes to us on Real Girls and we can get a Canadian broadcaster.

Our next chance is with a Canadian broadcaster and our project contact that both Brendan and Tony created.

I just opened my God file and reread the note I put in the God of My Understanding Box. In other words, I have a file that when I run into a problem and I can't seem to solve, I turn it over by putting it into my God File or God of My Understanding Box and letting go of the results.

How Do I Believe — If I Don't Believe?

There are those who say, "Fake it till you make it." Okay, but how do we reconcile believing that a power greater than ourselves, the Master Mind, can change our life? In my case, it has been experience. Plain and simple!

I ran on David Brady Power and self-will for a long time, until I was 39 years of age. The results? Not so good.

Quite frankly, having spent so much time in California, I always wished I could find a spiritual drive-through where I could go up to the window and say, "I'd like an order of peace of mind and a side order of serenity! And while you are at it, can you supersize those for me, please?" That's how my brain works.

Yes, I did accomplish a great deal in my business and creative life. However, I also found myself suffering from tremendous anxiety, doubt, and, at times, resentment.

As a teenager and a very young man, I had an allergy to alcohol. Every time I drank I broke out in a drunk and in spots: Like the Bahamas, New York City and other odd spots. The Irish in me I guess. I didn't realize alcoholism was a disease, analogous to type 2 diabetes. I inherited it. I realized at 21 years of age that I couldn't drink and for some reason I was able to stop. I did ask the God of my understanding at the time to help me stop that behavior. But, I was not willing to surrender any other part of my life to anything outside of myself because I just didn't have enough faith in a Power greater than me.

Here was the crux of my problem: I had always sought God or wisdom out there. In other words, it never dawned on me that I could have a Power greater than myself internally. It just seemed so odd and so foreign to my upbringing as a Catholic. I always thought in terms of "heaven" being in the "stratosphere." When you are a child in the Catholic Church, you are taught that the Holy Sacrament is kept on the altar in a tabernacle. It has a red candle burning beside it and we are raised to think of it in terms of the real "Body and Blood of Jesus."

However, as a six-year-old, I used to sit in church and stare at the tabernacle and think that there was a tunnel inside that led up to heaven, which in my childlike mind, was in the stratosphere.

Then I wondered, what about the Australians? Their "out there" is my "down there." Needless to say, the idea of a power greater than myself has been a lifelong journey of discovery for me.

I now feel as though I'm finally getting close to having an absolute faith that the Master Mind (or God, in my case) can change me. However, today I believe that the spark of Divinity, the very essence of what created the universe, is within each of us.

I have Michael Dowd, the author of *Thank God For Evolution*, to thank for that. His point: We are all made up of stardust. Every human being has, within his or her biology, the literal stardust created at the Big Bang.

All of a sudden, between his ideas and some others I was pursuing, it started to dawn on me. This idea is what the preachers, rabbis, imam's and ministers had always talked about when they said, "We were made in the image and likeness of God."

It's not literal. Does God have to go to the bathroom and defecate? Pardon my crudeness, but I doubt it. But, the spark of the Divine, that infinitesimal part of us that is made up from the "spark" of God, is within each of us.

In another interesting book, *Ancient Secrets*

of Success, Tulshi Sen points out that every drop of the ocean is the ocean. If we melt ice, how do we separate what was ice from what was the water? It all flows into one.

It is my belief today that we are the Divine Sparks of God manifested on this earth. And, it appears there are those who are so highly evolved that they can perform the miracles of the Bible. Suddenly, so much of what I'd learned made sense to me.

The good news today is I barely resemble the David Brady of my youth emotionally, spiritually, or physically. I have grown a great deal. And, without exception, every period of growth has been preceded by a period of intense discomfort, emotional pain, and often real financial challenges. I've never learned anything on a good day.

Facing the death and loss of my mother; having my second marriage end; losing the company I had started because I couldn't stay in it with a partner who was an active drug addict — each of these stopped me in my tracks. They made me take stock. When I lost my company, I realized that once again I'd set myself up to be hurt by going into business with people who couldn't be counted on to keep their word.

At the time, however, it was so incredibly painful that I felt like my life would end. And here is the truth! I am not alone. How many of you who are now reading this can relate in some way to some or one of the issues I'm raising?

Who hasn't been hurt by the loss of a loved one or a family member, been through the breakup of a marriage, or experienced difficulties in business? I don't think you would be normal if you said you hadn't. What I have to believe is that if I let go and let the Master Mind transform me, then I will create the best possible outcome.

It's like the fellow who, after falling off the

cliff and grabbing a branch of a tree sticking out of the rock face, with a thousand-foot fall below him, looks up and prays: "Dear God, please help me." The voice says, "Let Go and Trust." The fellow then looks up and says, "Is there anyone else up there?" Faith: it is not always easy to acquire. And it's especially not easy to come by if you are a humanist, agnostic, or atheist. It is even difficult if you are someone like me who has devoted a significant part of my life to being a seeker of the truth, inspiration, and a conscious contact with some form of Higher Power.

One of the challenges I have is in reconciling that it is okay to ask the Master Mind specifically for help. I'm one of those people who have been influenced by the concept that it's only okay to pray for knowledge of God's will and the power to carry that out. You dare not ask for anything for yourself.

That belief is in contrast and contradiction

to so many of the New Testament writings, and I use them as a demonstration to me that it is okay to ask. As an example, in Matthew 7:7 when he says, "Ask, and it shall be given you; seek, and you shall find; knock, and it shall be opened to you: For everyone that asks receives; and he that seeks finds; and to him that knocks it shall be opened. Or what man is there of you, whom if his son asks for bread, will he give him a stone?"

So, here I am, a litmus test for you the reader. By the time you finish this book, you will know whether I have come to believe that a power greater than myself, the Master Mind, can change my life. Or I will be in the proverbial toilet.

There is nothing I want more than to have my life changed. I no longer wish to feel the anxiety and fear of loss and financial insecurity that I am currently experiencing.

I also no longer desire to have to deal with individuals whose creative horizons consist of rednecks, rock stars on crack, or young women whose only claim to fame is to be the object of sensuality. In my view, there is nothing wrong with sensuality in the correct context. But, when it is one's primary purpose in life, that's not good. Those people will age too. (Although when I was young, I never thought it would happen to me!) The other challenge I face is that with all the work I've done, I'm stunned that I find myself here at this stage of my life. For years, I've been working to change, and, in fact, I have changed a great deal.

But, once again, my faulty filter is kicking in like a toddler having a tantrum. Perfectionism. I think that it has to be all or nothing, black or white thinking. It's counterproductive too, when I think like this.

I have changed. Are the changes going as quickly as I would like? No! One of my challenges in life is that I want everything now (patience not being a strong suit in those of us with my type of brain). When I was a young man of 20 or 21, I wanted what my then very affluent father-in-law had — a beautiful home with a pool, a Cadillac, and the ability to travel the world.

What I learned as an adult, and as I got to have many of the same things, is the amount of hard work that has to go into supporting this lifestyle. When people see my lifestyle from the outside, what they see is a man with a nice car, a home in the country, and a very comfortable apartment in midtown Toronto, who travels frequently between Toronto, California, and Europe.

Because I have a lot of flaws in my personality around faith, I don't have perfect faith. I've always been reluctant to trust that the concept of a Higher Power could change my life because I had quite a horrible experience with my father around being able to trust him.

As a result, I made the decision that I only would count on myself at a very young age to figure everything out. The only exception was my drinking when I was younger. As I said earlier, thankfully I was willing and able to ask for help with that issue, but not the other parts of my life.

So, the challenge is really to begin to trust that we are being taken care of. The good news is that I've come back from owing over $5 million dollars, and today I do have assets.

If I decide to shut my company down, it will be done in an organized fashion. I will make sure that everyone knows what I am doing and what my plan is. I do have resources to get by on, but I will have to right size my life. How did we come to this level of understanding? By asking for help today and believing that we are being guided to the best solution.

We also have to be open to change, which I wasn't, for the longest time. Letting go of old ideas is arguably the most difficult thing any of us ever undertakes. My mind (the faulty filter) is the evil twin brother to the dwarf Gimli from *Lord of the Rings*. He is the red-haired one that was always going into battle and is a mighty warrior.

His evil twin brother, the Toxic Dwarf, resides in my mind and says, "Loser. You are toast. Your life will never work out. Hurl yourself off the nearest high building."

Once again, when he starts up at 5:00 a.m., just when I first wake up, I now say, "Good morning. Thank you for sharing. You can have the day off."

Fortunately, I live in a bungalow in the country and only on the 5th floor of my building in Toronto. If I jumped, all I would do is render myself disabled. My mind is analogous to my computer booting up. Its default setting from growing up in an alcoholic home is things are not predictable or stable. Always be vigilant and aware of potential danger. Always worry because you don't know what is coming next. Be hyperaware of your environment. Be terrified of making a mistake.

Those are all perfectionist traits, which are not healthy. A psychiatrist once said to my friend, "Perfectionism is the highest form of self-abuse." We can do a lifetime of psychotherapy, one-on-one counseling, or intensive group therapy. All can support you in seeking a solution.

As well, you can have a Master Mind group and ask for help connecting with a Higher Power, or simply ask for guidance and the gift of belief. If we do believe it, we can achieve it.

We can overcome countless character defects, or flaws if you will. We can change our lives from ones of quiet desperation to lives that are much more pleasant and, dare I say, joy-filled. Does this mean you will be tiptoeing through the tulips on a daily basis? Probably not on a daily basis, but, undoubtedly your life will be much more manageable. If we believe that the Master Mind will change our life, and we humbly ask for guidance and direction to do its will, the chances are that in some odd way we will find our life unexplainably correcting itself. Problems that used to plague us will begin to straighten out.

Unexpected solutions will appear, and we will see opportunities where we once saw problems. We can also stop having to think that we've done something wrong. We haven't. It is just a fact that life is difficult much of the time, and when we try to deal with it alone, it is lonely and isolating.

Asking for help and expecting positive results will bring about change, change that will increase when we utilize the concept of the Master Mind or Divine Mind to assist us.

Furthermore, the great news is that you can create a conscious contact with the Master

Mind of your choice. It's your private concept, so you can let go of old stereotypes and ask yourself, "If I could have a personal relationship with the Master Mind or Higher Power of my choice, what would that look like?" In my case, I started thinking about the possibility of having a friend with whom I could talk, versus buddy with the beard. In my juvenile mind, I saw God with a large clipboard, sitting on his throne keeping track of the 7.1 billion people on earth. Making sure He knows who has been naughty or nice.

I also let go of my old idea that I was not worthy of having a connection with a Higher Power because I was so flawed. I also surrendered the idea that any self-respecting Higher Power would blow me off because I am so damaged. I no longer think that. But how many of us believe and feel that? They even have a section in the Catholic Mass at Communion where you say, "Lord, I'm not worthy."

With all due respect, my sense is you are worthy. I believe this because the spark of Divinity created you and you are "God's or the Master Mind or Divine Mind's" daughter or son. How would you treat your children? With love and respect, I would hope

Chapter Seven

I Am Ready To Be Changed

STEP 3. I AM READY TO BE CHANGED

I realize that erroneous self-defeating thinking is the cause of my problems, unhappiness, fears, and failures. I am ready to be changed so my life can be transformed.

I'm sitting in Toronto now, at my apartment on Avenue Road. It is July 29, 2013.

We're in the middle of a very severe heat wave. I have the air conditioner going full tilt. It's about a quarter to four in the afternoon. I've just had some toast, a coffee, and a quick lie down to get my energy up.

I love summer. I've always loved summer, probably because I was born on May 29th. I feel that we all love the season we were born in. It is just an observation on my part, with absolutely no empirical data to back that up.

One of my beliefs is that I am not intelligent enough, talented enough, good enough, handsome enough, or lucky enough to have certain things go my way.

I don't think all of these thoughts at once. They emerge within the context of my personal and interpersonal relationships and situations in life. In spite of the fact that I have a wall full of awards and that I have produced a lot of television and four feature films, my mind tells me it was just a fluke. Luck. Faulty filter again.

My Childhood Discovery About Charm

Where does this thinking come from? Childhood. In my case, I misinterpreted what was said to me as a child. So little was understood when I was just a kid growing up in the mid-

1950s. I started Grade 1 in 1953. I was six years of age. In my first book, *Transforming Childhood Trauma, 8 Spiritual Steps to Reclaim Your Life,* I told the story of the Grey Nun in Timmins (my hometown) who took me into the cloakroom because I lied to her on the second day of school. I didn't want to go to school. I was terrified.

It was in that cloakroom where I saw a black and green flag that had a big elephant on it. I said, "What's that, Sister?" as she was getting ready to give me the strap for lying. She looked at it and said, "Dumbo the Safety Elephant. He's there to help you stay out of trouble."

I looked up with my big blue eyes and said extemporaneously, "Oh Dumbo, where are you now?" She burst out laughing and did something that astounded me. She slapped her hand and then said, "Don't ever lie to me again." I don't think I ever did after that. It was at that moment I realized that I could make people laugh, and I would go on to use that as a defense mechanism for a great part of my life.

I didn't have a great role model in my father. As I was growing up, his alcoholism was escalating. Now, I don't blame my father for how my life turned out. But he did influence me significantly, and his behavior did have an impact on all of us growing up in that violent, alcoholic home. They call it dysfunctional today. What did I hear? There were fighting and emotional altercations between my mother and father. There was the threat of physical violence from my dad toward several of my siblings. There was always tension in the air. Somehow, I got it into my head that it was my fault.

It is now the last week of July 2013 and I am overwhelmed with fear of Monday morning.

I've never worked so hard to close a deal. We have so many projects out. Will we hear this week on Contact, Myth Hunters, CANUSA Lodge, and

Rock Club. The stress is unbelievable. I keep praying and asking for guidance. I need to let go. It's really difficult

One of the many challenges I'm having about being willing to change is not to let my unhealthy old self-defeating thinking take hold. As I said previously, and it's worth repeating, when my faulty filter kicks in my mind say, "It's too late." In my thinking, it is darkest before the dawn. However, I've been here before on several occasions. Last night I spoke to Dennis, Father John, and Ron. We had dinner at Dave's Road House in Prince Edward County.

It's become apparent to me that I'm holding onto my ego. While I'm willing, or I say I'm willing to let go, am I? Apparently not! As I indicated earlier, I am always willing to let go of my drinking problem. I'm also always willing to ask my Higher Power to take care of my children. But hold on — "my business"? I don't think so.

Another three days have passed. I can feel the tension mounting in me. I keep wondering, okay, what am I doing wrong? What is it that I'm not doing, right? Tony is away, and I'm here alone. I've never prayed so hard in my entire life.

I've made the decision to drive down to my house in the country and ride out what I'm going through there. Tony is heading for a holiday with his father. I told him that he needed to be prepared not to come back to work if we can't close new business. I have to start thinking about alternative plans. I really have to think about letting go and shutting down my apartment at 585 Avenue Road and just working out of my house.

Let me paraphrase the late great "gonzo journalist," Hunter S. Thompson, who said, "The film and television business are a cruel, shallow money trench run by pimps and whores and where good men die like dogs: then there is also a downside to it."

Start the Change

What are the steps I need to take once I ask to be changed? In many cases, our problems are financial. How do we find a solution that will work across the board if we have little or no experience with the business of finance?

As a business, we all need to create a spending plan or a budget. We also need to have an accurate list of our income. And it must be accurate. If you have $1,000 a month coming in, that's what you have. If you have $5,000 coming in, that is what you must plan for. If you have $10,000 a month coming in and are spending $15,000 a month, you are headed for a day of reckoning and a world of hurt.

Many people have magical thinking (I might be included in this category at times) and they keep spending savings trying to maintain a lifestyle that will eventually leave them insolvent, depressed, and even suicidal.

However, if you are in good health and you are ambulatory, then in this day and age there are many positions open to those retirees that were not open a decade or two ago. This same concept will also apply to those who are middle-aged and perhaps find themselves downsized or laid off. What is your hobby? Do you love carpentry or decorating? Do you have a passion for renovating?

Check out the large big box stores in the numerous plazas that might need folks who know what they are doing. How about writing? You can earn $25 an hour if you look for opportunities such as writing for Direct Mail businesses. How about students needing tutoring?

Were you a manager or an executive in your other life? Community colleges and universities are facing retiring professors who are boomers who've done this all their lives. But teaching can be new and exciting for those of us who come to this calling later in life. If your mind says like mine did, "Hold on, Dave, you were a big shot producer. Do you want people to see you now working for a wage?" I say to my mind, "Thank you for sharing." Once again the ego (edge good out) gets in there and starts to rear his (in my case) toxic self and passing judgment on what it is I'm thinking of doing. I simply say, "Thank you for sharing, now kindly screw off."

Being ready to change can include having to rethink or change our career path and recreate our finances to match a new lifestyle. This idea is very difficult if you must make what you perceive as a downward move. You may have been a CEO or a vice president of a large organization when you found yourself out of work. You may have owned your own business when you had to declare personal or corporate bankruptcy. An alcohol or drug problem may have removed you from your position as a professional, and now you must rebuild your life from the ground up.

Don't let your mind stand in the way of you possibly having the best time of your life. Imagine little or no stress, no massive responsibility and just the chance to be a regular guy or gal that gets to meet people and find out just how wonderful they are. And of course, there will always be the occasional challenging person whom we can thank for helping us learn tolerance. There are many opportunities today to set you up as a consultant. The same with chain stores where the focus is art if you have any talent as a fine artist, potter, designer, or teacher. It gets you out, and you meet new people.

If you go through this kind of "right sizing" you will need to examine your finances. When you create what I call your spending plan (or budget if you feel better using that term) you will need to create one that will allow you to have fun and include an amount dedicated to entertainment. You will also want to have an amount to take care of your basic needs and keep something in reserve in the event that you need outside help to keep your home clean. If you have grandchildren or adult children, save a small amount so you can visit with your children or grandkids.

It is very important to have a little money — $50 to $200 a month for such things as massages, counseling, or chiropractic treatment that help with your overall well-being and self-care. Please don't isolate yourself either. For many of us, being isolated is going to be a major problem, especially when we've lost our friends or a loved one. We cannot sit in our homes and just vegetate. First, it will hasten our departure from the planet through a myriad of related maladies, and second, it will probably bring on a great deal of loneliness and depression.

In cities like Toronto, Los Angeles, New York, London, Sydney, Vancouver, Nashville, and Calgary, and I am assuming other large cities, there will be schools teaching massage. They will offer such treatments at a greatly reduced rate for training their massage therapists. It will also introduce you to self-care, a concept many of us overachievers are totally unfamiliar with. "What a waste of time" will probably be the first thought that crosses your mind. "**Faulty Filter**." In 2013 I calculated what you would need to retire in the USA (these numbers may have changed slightly since then):

Retirement Statistics	Data
Average retirement age	62
Average length of retirement	18 years
Average savings of a 50-year-old	$43,797
Total cost for a couple over 65 to pay for medical treatment over a 20-year span	$215,000
Percentage of people ages 30-54 who believe they will not have enough money put away for retirement	80%
Percentage of Americans over 65 who rely completely on Social Security	35%

Percentage of Americans who don't save anything for retirement	36%
Total number of Americans who turn 65 per day	6,000
Percentage of population that is 65 years of age or older	13%
Out of 100 people who start working at the age of 25, by the age 65:	
Will be considered wealthy	1%
Have adequate capital stowed away for retirement	4%
Will still be working	3%
Are dependent on Social Security, friends, relatives or charity	63%
Are dead	29%
Americans older than 50 account for:	
Percent of all financial assets	77%
Percent of total consumer demand	54%
Prescription drug purchases	77%
All over-the-counter drugs	61%
Auto Sales	47%
All luxury travel purchases	80%

Amount Needed in Savings for Retirement		
Monthly Income Needed	**Savings Needed for 20 Years**	**Savings Needed for 30 Years**
$1,000	$166,696	$212,150

$2,000	$333,392	$424,300
$3,000	$500,087	$636,450
$4,000	$666,783	$848,601
$5,000	$833,479	$1,060,751
$6,000	$1,000,175	$1,272,901
$7,000	$1,166,871	$1,485,051
$8,000	$1,333,567	$1,697,201
$9,000	$1,500,262	$1,909,351
$10,000	$1,666,958	$2,121,501

The above sums assume your portfolio will earn a 6% annualized return during the course of your retirement and endure 2% annual inflation erosion.

We in Canada are blessed with universal healthcare, which eliminates over $200,000 from our costs. If you don't fit comfortably into one of the above categories, what can you do to survive? That's the question. The answer is acceptance. Otherwise, you are left with feelings of failure, low self-esteem, and hopelessness. Are you ready to be changed and let go of old erroneous self-defeating thinking? Acceptance can be a very difficult task to undertake.

But you don't need to be alone. No one does. We are all worthy human beings. We are not our bank accounts, although it is a lot easier to be spiritual when you have a positive bank balance. It is also valuable to be active in a spiritual setting like a church or fellowship of some kind where you are with positive, like-minded people. There are so many support groups today for every imaginable situation in life. And the more you can share openly and honestly with others, the less is the emotional burden on yourself. As far as finances, the fact is there are probably more people in financial need than there are who are financially solvent. So clearly I need to let go and let God take away this unhealthy and self-defeating thinking, and I make a commitment to you that I will do this today.

It is just so uncomfortable for me. I find it difficult to let go of control. That feeling that I am in control is just so deeply ingrained in me. It is like making the decision to bungee jump off that super skyscraper in Dubai — your stomach comes out of your mouth, it's so terrifying. I saw it on the last *Mission Impossible* — 18 or 105 — whichever one it was.

In Conclusion

Are you ready to be changed? Are you going to try and figure out how we will survive? But we can do this.

People who have contracted severe or life-threatening illnesses may believe this kind of thinking is rubbish. However, all one has to do is go on the Internet and Google how negative thinking affects our health or the correlation between negative thinking and disease. It will astound you to see just how much our old self-defeating thinking does affect us, and the outcome of our medical treatments. It has been proven time and time again in these empirical medical studies that our thinking has a significant bearing on the outcome of our treatment, especially if one has been prone to self-pity, anger, resentment, or jealousy most of their lives. These emotions are poison to our system, and we need to let go of them, and the sooner, the better.

Chapter Eight

I Decide To Be Changed

STEP 4. I DECIDE TO BE CHANGED

I make a decision to surrender my will and my life to the Master Mind. I ask to be changed at depth.

Facing Financial Challenges

If you don't have the resources to live independently, then you are in the company of roughly three-quarters of North Americans who don't have enough. Take heart, you are not alone. We have to come up with a new paradigm for aging and living quality lives by reallocating resources in an intelligent way. We have to, or the societal, physical, and emotional costs are going to be staggering.

We're not all going to be spending the winter in Florida, California, or some other sunny place. But, with a group of friends, using some old-fashioned ingenuity, we may be able to come up with some alternatives. What about doing something like finding a car service where they pay you to drive a car from whatever city you are in to Florida, California, or Arizona? You could spend a week or two enjoying the warm weather thereby cutting your costs and sharing a place just like you did when you were young.

Even if you can't, it doesn't mean you are worthless or a burden. We all have gifts, regardless of our financial circumstances, especially if we have a positive mental attitude, an ability to go with the flow and seek guidance in our lives when we feel powerless. That is being changed at depth.

We have to alter our view of family, aging, and what it means to allow future generations to age with dignity. It has only been in the last generation that the idea of not caring for the elderly within the family has taken precedent. It was those of us — we boomers — who blew our aging parents off, metaphorically, and in some cases, literally.

I'm afraid that, for many of us, we're about to discover that as we do unto others, it is done unto us. When we are young, we feel invincible. We feel independent. We want what we want, and we want it now. To a large degree, we have become a very self-centered, selfish generation who are about to pay the price for our lack of caring. And it's going to be brutal if we don't shift our view to taking care of others and asking to be changed at depth. As it turns out there are many universal laws that we thought we could flaunt in our younger years, and now they've come home to roost. Didn't see that coming, did we?

So, what is the answer? What is our hope?

Well, one of the tools we can use to help us get back on course is the Eight Steps. We all need company and support. We all need love and compassion. Let's begin practicing with each other — even when we're occasionally upset with those closest to us.

August 15, 2013

I'm sitting on an Air Canada flight in Executive First Class. This is a complete gift to me as I'm on a real discount airfare. However, I was up at 4 a.m. to catch this flight to Vancouver. I simply asked for an aisle seat, and they bumped me to First Class. Yeah Air Canada! I'm on this flight because while meditating I had a thought, "Why not see if one of the universities in Vancouver would consider having you teach in their film program?" And there was a notice for a part-time teaching position. Ten hours per week.

I've done it before very successfully. I've had a written goal that I want to move back to West Vancouver for years now. I did put an add on one of the Internet sites. As a result I was able to rent my furnished house for three months, the length of the teaching contract. I'm one of three people being interviewed tomorrow. I have no idea if I will get it or not.

I've been totally open with my banks and creditors. Here's the miracle. Once I accepted that shutting down was inevitable, a calm came over me. And I had no idea if I would get the position, but I could only try.

Self-Defeating Thinking

Here is what I knew on that day on that flight. Three weeks ago my old self-defeating thinking took over, and I couldn't see a way out of where I was. I felt hopeless and defeated.

I mentioned this to my close friends that night at Dave's Road House, I was feeling hopeless and that life may not be worth living and they managed to talk me through the process. That kind of thinking is disastrous not only to me but also to my children and my family as well. They just worry themselves over my mental attitude. In our willingness to be changed, we have to be rigorously honest with ourselves. That is how I felt. I was shocked, sitting and reflecting on the airplane that I felt that way. But I did. And, now it's gone. I'm feeling quite good. More and more, things are turning around right now.

However, my old self-defeating thinking reappears: "David, you are not good enough; you are not smart enough; talented enough; funny enough; young enough to be hired by a university. What about your age? Who are you trying to kid?" These were the thoughts I initially had when I sent the email out to the university.

Actually, I sent two in a row because I tried to write one while I was in a meeting. My ex-wife always said to me (and I said this in the second email), "David, you are a man. Men can't do two things at the same time. Please learn to accept that." Damn, she's right.

Here are the facts: I have a wealth of real world experience. I am a rock solid teacher with tremendous experience both in and out of the classroom. I've been blessed with a real gift of communication. I also enjoy being around young people as they are so full of energy and enthusiasm and remind me of myself when I was their age.

I am, according to my children, a wonderful man who cares a lot about people. They have also told me that their friends love coming to our office and hanging out with us. They think I'm cool. That's so funny to me, but in a warm way.

We are constantly having students around

our productions because I believe in mentoring them. I can remember how difficult it was for us when we started out. I can still remember the few "Hollywood-type" producers and directors who would take the time to speak to us as though we were human beings and not a pain-in-the-ass.

So there I was, sitting on the plane preparing my lecture, which was to be part of the interview process, "What is a story?" I could easily be depressed if I wasn't to get the job tomorrow. But, at this moment, I was feeling fairly positive because regardless of what was to happen, I was willing to let go of all that unhealthy thinking that had caused me so many problems in the past. I was willing to let go and trust that my new Master Mind centered thinking would allow me to find solutions to my problems that I've not had before.

Learning to Trust the Master Mind

It had only been three weeks since I realized there was a solution out of the mess I was in. I did an inventory, and realized, okay, I have a house. I have equity. I have savings and investments: I'm not going to starve today, even though my mind (faulty filter) believes it will. I am ready to believe that my life can be transformed, and I am now ready to let go and let my Higher Power change me.

I believe that I am being guided to my greatest good. Even though I can't see it at this very moment, there is no problem that can't be solved by trusting in my Higher Power.

One of my other concerns is that I also have a residence in Toronto. Do I give it up? Do I keep it when I sell my house? And there was still one last hope for production.

10:00 a.m. August 15, 2013
We were just turned down by USA Network on my CANUSA Lodge. I will write it as a novel I think. So, that leaves us with a potential six hours on a series called Contact.

If it comes through I've decided that I will turn the production over to Mike, who has been with me for almost seven years. I will also have my son, Brendan, and Tony be the primary source of creativity.

As I may have said before, I have a friend with whom I've worked for many years, and she can direct at least three of them. I might direct the other three

It's 5:45 on August 15, 2013

I'm sitting looking at Horseshoe Bay, British Columbia. I have just taken a picture of one of the most beautiful sights one can ever see. The cloud-covered peaks of the Coastal Range and the harbor in the background. It's starting to rain, so I guess I will get back to the car and continue my writing in a café. I've just had dinner at Troll's Fish N Chips.

It is a landmark in Horseshoe Bay and has been since 1946. I've decided to sit in the rain and enjoy nature. Tonight I will hang out to stay awake so I will sleep in until at least 6 or 7 tomorrow morning.

So, becoming ready to be changed. Today I saw a beautiful apartment in West Vancouver on Bellevue. This is the street that runs along the shoreline of the Pacific Ocean and looks over English Bay from West Vancouver. It is a little on the expensive side. The good news is, the manager said he's flexible. I will see what they say tomorrow at the university.

Before the interview, I read over my notes. I am hoping sincerely that the research, the reading, and the writing that I've done will lead me to a place of being able to demonstrate to the faculty members that I know what I am doing. I am anxious to do the best job possible. At least I've taken the time to prepare. However, unlike in the old days, I'm perfectly okay letting go and trusting that I will be guided to change so that my life can be transformed. I am so hopeful that my life will change. Sitting here in one of the most beautiful locations on earth makes me realize how much I want to live here. A huge seagull has landed about six feet from me and is just sitting on the railing looking at me. It's as if it's welcoming me back home.

A sizeable BC Ferry is just pulling out from Horseshoe Bay and heading over to Nanaimo, the city where my sister Trish and her husband, Chris, live. I will be back here Tuesday to have lunch with them.

The rain has passed. The clouds are lying in layers, like giant blankets in mid air — and rising above the verdant mountainside. Beautiful. It is just so beautiful here in British Columbia. In the past, I would seldom sit and just enjoy the beauty of nature. I was always in too big a hurry, too busy as I always had to be somewhere. I am committed to letting go and trusting that I will be guided to the next right steps.

I received an email today from my financial partner. He wants to talk to me in person. I understand that too. He has been such a gentleman.

I have a lot on my plate. I truly recognize that I must stay in the day. When I think about tomorrow, I lose the peace of this moment. When I think of yesterday and all the things I didn't accomplish, I become distracted and miss the beauty surrounding me. Right now, right here I have enough. I am good enough. I am so grateful to be here. One of my greatest challenges is to accept myself as I am. I am not perfect.

Friday, August 16, 2013 Vancouver, BC

I have an interview at the university. It is at 3:15 today. I've just gone over my lecture again. It's 6:15 in the morning. I did get to sleep in by staying awake last night even though my body thinks it's 9:15 with the time change.

Again, I'm sitting this morning thinking this is odd, as I've never really gone for an interview before. When I taught in the past, they were just happy to have me come down and teach. This is getting a real job. I feel pretty good about the material. If I'm successful, it's because I took the time to prepare. If I don't, it's because I'm not the right person for the job. Not because I've done something wrong. That is a healthy change for me. How do I move out here so quickly? If we don't get our 6-hour series, I have to give notice on my apartment in Toronto and pay one more month's rent, but do I want to make two drives across Canada? I don't think so, although I'm going to have to drive my car out if I don't haul it out on the back of a moving truck.

So, I am trying to approach this differently than I would have in the past. Perhaps I can seek some feedback from folks who've had to make these moves. I thought, just get rid of apartment furniture. I will go online and see how much a truck is from Toronto to Vancouver. If I had to do that twice, it would be brutal.

I will wait until the house sells and just pick up some used furniture in Vancouver. I will put my things into storage. I am ready to be changed and let go of my old self-defeating thinking. I will hear from the university soon.

Romance

Romance is one area where I don't feel

qualified to speak, given my track record. Nonetheless, I have to look at where else am I ready to change. Romantic relationships have been a challenge for me. I may not be alone. However, in the case of Deb, we were married for 20 years. We are still very close, but it took a great deal of work to get through it. With my first wife, we were kids having kids. As I mentioned earlier, Bev wasn't even out of her teens when our son was born. What is interesting, and makes me think that there may be something to the old karmic wheel, is what has happened to me with my relationship in the States.

Here is what I would do all the time in the past. From the ages of 23 to 39, until I got remarried, I knew at least three women who had strong feelings for me. But I was focused on my career in the film business and traveled all the time. In each case, these women would express their affection for me, and I'd say the very thing that was just said to me. I'm not interested in getting married. I'm not interested in a domestic situation. I've been on my own for "X" number of years, and I like it. But if you want to keep it casual, and we could see each other once in a while, that would be good.

The difference is that today I do want to meet someone I can love and be with. But I am grateful for the time I had with my friend for the two and a half years we saw each other. She is a wonderful woman with a great family. And now I've experienced the pain of that loss and, of course being a man, I was a complete idiot. The question I have to ask myself is, When will I ever learn?

One of the humorous things near the end of my being single at 39 is that I was seeing two women, one in NYC and one in LA. I told both of them about the other, as I always prided myself on being upfront and honest. Well, they got together. Ouch!!!! Talk about getting caught in the crossfire.

However, I'm close to both of them today, or at least I've visited with both of them. They seem to have forgiven me for being such a complete jerk (which I was back then). Ironically, my friend Celeste, who is one of these women, just called me the other day, and she confirmed that I was a very decent human being. Nice. We can all laugh about it today.

Wednesday. August 28, 2013 6:00 p.m.
Originally, they were going to do all the interviews on Friday, but one was postponed until today. So, I will not know today as I had hoped. In the meantime, I was able to contact the former chair of Ryerson University where I taught, and he's written a very strong letter of support for me.
I've received a beautiful letter from my longtime friend and associate George Flak. It

almost brought me to tears, as his description of me is just so generous and caring.

ursday, August 29, 2013 10 p.m.

I am at my house in Sandhurst, Ontario, with my brother Robert. My good friends Dennis and Paula just live east of the Ferry, and they are two of the folks I really depend on for emotional and spiritual support.

I spend a great deal of my time in Picton, which is in "the County" as it is affectionately referred to. I love this part of Eastern Ontario, and I always said to people it's because it's as close as I can get to the West Coast.

I just received the call from the search committee, and I've been offered the position in Vancouver.

I need to be in Vancouver on Tuesday September 3rd. Dear God in Heaven. How am I going to do this?

It's what I had hoped for. It's also looking like what I'm preaching does work. That's really encouraging. It would have been very embarrassing not to have these steps work.

I can't even begin to put into words what this week has been like. It's been three days since I got the call.

If I never believed in the power of the Master Mind before, I do now. My ex-wife Deb will help organize my move out of 585 Avenue Road. I have talked to Tony, my former assistant, and he will organize the physical move of the furniture into storage so my son, Brendan, can have it on his return from Vancouver.

I've taken my car in to get new tires and to get new brakes as driving through the mountains can be dangerous

The two young women who are graduate

students at Queen's and the University of Toronto in electrical engineering are moving into my house today as I'm on my way up to Toronto this afternoon with my car packed full of clothes, and I have more there to pick up. Wow. I am feeling so much stress just trying to figure out how to get all this done in a matter of two days

It Really Works!

My friend Pete, who works at Ontario Power Generating, has posted on the company bulletin board that my house is up for sale. I got word that they are going to build the new power plant just east of my home. There will be new folks moving into the area, and someone will like it. I have done a great deal of renovation work on the house.

Stress While Asking for Change

Let's talk about stress. How much stress do I think I have? Mega stress, meta-stress, the stress of stress? What about all the possible challenges trying to move to Vancouver with five days' notice? I will have to move from not one, but two homes in two different cities — my house in the country and my place in Toronto. Combine that with not knowing about my company's future and, boy, do I feel stress.

I have committed to making the decision to be changed, and I am surrendering my will and my life to the Master Mind. I ask to change at depth. Okay, it's been about fifteen seconds. There has been no angelic choir singing in my head. There was a flash of light a few days ago on the flight back from Vancouver, but it was when the captain turned the plane to starboard and we got a glimpse of the rising sun. However, I did get a sense of excitement.

Practically speaking, what does this all

mean? First and foremost, I made the decision over 13 months ago really to try a version of this Step. I made a commitment to a group of friends that I was going to try surrendering and seeking my Higher Power's will in my life. Do I know who this Divine Power is? No! But, if there is one, I'm sure He/She/It knows me. Since then I have asked every day to be changed. I've learned to be careful what you pray for as you might get it, and change can be both frightening and uncomfortable.

I have made this point before, but it is imperative I let go of old ideas. Letting go is not as easy as it sounds. Whenever you make a declaration to change certain behaviors in your life, have you ever noticed that the very things you want to change seem to appear right in front of your face?

I ask for patience, and I'm surrounded by slow pokes in traffic. I realize that I'm the one sitting there fuming while a nice couple is just out for a drive. I'm pounding on my steering wheel because I have to get the car home so I can sit down and read my emails. Hello! The aforementioned is not critical. Or, I worry endlessly and needlessly. I obsess whether someone likes a project that I've created. I am powerless over the fact that my life as I knew it before the assault is over. I have flare-ups of anger at times because I feel life is unfair. The fact is life is unfair a lot of the time. I need to surrender this behavior and all my self-defeating thinking to the Master Mind. It is my only hope for real peace of mind and happiness. More importantly, I need to let go of old thinking around money, property, and prestige. It is something I'm still very attached to at times. However, as I alluded to earlier, I need to get right-sized about it. I'm no longer going to have a couple of residences for the time being. My very nicely renovated home with the comfortable deck on which I could sit and watch the water, and the birds, is going. But, it's my choice.

> *August 30, 2013 Toronto*
>
> *I've had to really let go of results in that area with over 300 executives saying "no" to me. I am powerless over their decisions, and my ego wants to me to strike out at them for doing their jobs. It does feel unfair. If I had failed on a bunch of projects, that would be one thing. But I haven't.*
>
> *How willing am I to be changed? I seem to have run out of options in that area, and I'm down to the last possibility for now with potential productions. Could it change? Absolutely. Will it change? I have no idea at this moment.*

I just spoke to a network executive who once worked for me. He is now at one of the major channels. I asked him, "What about the proposal I handed you?" I told him, "I need you to be honest." He said, "Okay, it's just like everyone else's. I've got three ideas that are exactly the same. There is nothing in the idea you submitted that will make it stand out, like yours used to." There it is. Proof that my brain is damaged. I always was able to knock these proposals out of the park. Time and time again. Where does this leave me?

So, how do I make the decision to be changed? By letting go of the need to control. It is very interesting letting go of control and outcomes. Every part of me wants to rebel at this concept; my whole life I've always felt that if I don't take control, take charge, no one will be able to do what needs to get done. In my own case, I began changing when I hired a very competent young man about seven years ago. While he's not perfect, he is incredibly capable and intelligent. I can trust him to make good decisions.

I don't know about any of you who are reading this book, but I need to recognize that the endless chatter that is going on in my mind is just a complete waste of time and energy: *"moving, money, Vancouver, Toronto, Sandhurst, my relationship that's gone south on me, my health, aging, car repairs, selling the house, not selling the house, death, the dentist, writing this book, wanting to be of service, will I ever get laid again? Maybe some apple pie with ice cream, hoping I do well in the teaching position, telling them I really want this."*

The endless chatter just keeps rolling along basically in one variation or another of the aforementioned. I just have to stay in the habit of thanking my mind for sharing when it starts on this rampage.

If I am to be successful doing this Step, I must step out in faith. I must be willing to turn the results over to the Master Mind while also be willing to do the work myself. In other words, I can't just sit around thinking, "Okay, here is my order God, can I have it by Friday?"

As an example, what just happened to me? A few weeks ago I made the sincere declaration "I want to change my life and myself." What did I do to accomplish that?

First, I had to have a goal and declare it. Then I had to take action and move toward it. As I was meditating, I had the overwhelming sense to go online and check for a teaching position. When I saw that there was an opening at a university, I couldn't believe it. I had to write a letter expressing my desire to teach. When the woman called me the following week to say they wanted to interview me, I had to buy the plane ticket to fly out to Vancouver. Then I had to make a call to my second oldest friend, who just happens to live in Vancouver, to see if anyone had a place at which I could stay. He suggested I call another old friend. When I did telephone Tim, he said he would be away that week and was happy to have me stay in his condo/studio in Vancouver. Tim also left me his Smart car. It all just fell into place.

I did the planning and turned the results over to the Master Mind. It seems to have gone effortlessly. I found a potential residence where I could leave a deposit until Friday of that week. In the event that I don't get the teaching position, I will be able to get my deposit back. If I do get it, I have secured a place to live.

What I learned from that experience is that, if I'm willing to ask to be changed at depth and to turn my will and life over to the Master Mind, I will be guided to the best possible outcome. This is what I ask for every day now.

It's obviously easy to be changed at depth when everything is going your way. It's not when all you hear is no, and all you seem to experience is disappointment. It is baffling to me. Yet what I do know is that people have this faith, and those who desire to be changed at depth are happier human beings, even when things are not going their way! They have faith that it will turn around.

This is one of the things that I find interesting about researchers in the social or behavioural sciences. They usually don't take into account that people of faith have a measurable quality of life that is vastly different from people who do not.

I want to be changed. I don't want to be plagued by fear and doubt anymore. I don't want to lie awake at night wondering, "Will I end up penniless, homeless, alone? Will I ever find anyone to love who will love me back unconditionally? Will I ever find true peace of mind? Will I be able to repay my investors and creditors from my production company?"

These are questions that I am now asking to have guidance about by being changed at depth. I no longer want to do what I've done in the past that led to some pretty uncomfortable situations

I have changed a great deal as I said in the previous chapter. I've not had a drink of alcohol in over 45 years, and I've not touched a mood altering substance in nearly 30 years. I've stopped being a "rage-a-holic" decades ago, and stopped being irresponsible at the same time. I have saved money. I have repaid an enormous amount of debt and have cleared up the wreckage of my past, by and large.

I know I can change. That said, this is like the Ph.D. of letting go and surrendering. While I was always willing to ask the Master Mind to help me, I still kept running the show. It was not a conscious decision: I just didn't realize that this is what I was doing. Now I know and actually hope to be able to let go completely, and really just trust that every part of my life will work out, regardless of what the short term looks like. And I sincerely hope this includes letting go of life when the time comes to die. I know that it will come eventually and that I must make friends with death. Not in a macabre way but in the realization that death is a natural part of living that we all must pass through.

What I find interesting is that since I did make that decision 13 or 14 months ago, my life has taken a free fall into uncertainty.

Consider the old adage, "Be careful what you pray for." As with any journey in life, we must all confront our demons if we are ever to overcome them. As Joseph Campbell talks about in the *Hero's Journey,* we first have to come face to face with our single greatest enemy, our mind (ego), and overcome both the internal and external challenges of life.

To review: It is now September 10, 2013. Wow! Time is flying by. I'm sitting in my very comfortable apartment in West Vancouver. On my first day at university last Wednesday, September 3rd, there was a torrential downpour. I got soaked when I didn't know where to park and where I left my car was about 10 minutes from the building where I was to be. But I dried out in time for commencement gathering. Lesson one: It rains a lot in Vancouver. Bring an umbrella and raincoat.

Since then it has been sunny and warm. Outside my window in West Vancouver I can look at English Bay and see right across to UBC. There are numerous ships moored in the harbor. This is one of the most beautiful cities on earth, if not the most beautiful. I can see the mountains of Vancouver Island in the distance.

I have had to organize and move so much in such a short time. How did it work out? So far, so good! I've tried not to be the way I was in the past and worry so much. I keep simply letting go of expectations and observing my mind.

I am such a chronic worrier. How will I get everything into the apartment by myself? I asked to be changed at depth and then I ask for help. The two young men who take care of this building are only too happy to help me unload my car.

People were amazed that I was doing this trip alone with my car so fully packed, the only room in it was for me to sit in the driver's seat.

Every spare inch (or centimeter ... I am Canadian) was overflowing with personal things I would most need. The upside was I got to see some of the most beautiful sights I've ever seen. I love the Midwest, and the folks were just so incredibly friendly. I love America. I really do.

By letting go of worry, I did move two places. I did let go of my apartment in Toronto. I did manage to pack what I needed to survive in Vancouver until I could either move my furniture out from Sandhurst or sell my house furnished (which has not happened yet). Thank God for IKEA. I've got all I need to make it through now. I've also been able to see a lot of very old friends whom I knew as a young man in the 1970s and 1980s when I first moved to Vancouver. At this very moment, the question we have is practically speaking, How do we ask to be changed at depth?

First, we need a Master Mind group, those like-minded folks whom we can count on to support us through this process. We want to get a new perspective on our life. With their support, we can sit down and write out a gratitude list. Is your health good? Do you have a family that you speak to and are on good terms with and you can talk with about the past and how you are changing?

Do you have a few good friends? Do you have a nice place to live? Are you married? Do you have children? Do you have a pet that loves you? Are you connected to any community either through a hobby or church? Do you live in a beautiful place? And whenever things don't go our way, it's not personal. The universe doesn't have it in for you or me.

In my case, so many wonderful things have happened in my life. I've loved the fact I've been able to travel the world and meet some of the most interesting people alive. They have included world-renowned scientists, members of the

British Royal Family, a few Canadian prime ministers, Hollywood stars, and legends of Rock & Roll. However, it has not given me the peace of mind or happiness that I want. It has been exciting. It has also been interesting. It certainly has given me a lot of great stories to share with my students.

Chapter Nine

I Forgive

STEP 5. I FORGIVE

I forgive myself for all my mistakes and shortcomings. I also forgive all other persons who may have harmed me.

If ever there were a difficult principle to practice, forgiveness has to be it. When we have resentment or are angry with someone for what we perceive they've done to us, we tie up all of our life's energy. If we're unwilling to forgive them and accept them just the way they are, we're in for a heap of trouble.

I love the line about resentment — I drink poison and wait for the other guy to die. Does this mean we accept the inappropriate behavior? Absolutely not!

We have a responsibility to ourselves and

others, especially our children and grandchildren, to protect them from any form of abusive behavior, whether it is physical, emotional, sexual, or psychological.

We live in a society that suggests revenge is a dish best served cold. We are inundated with mass media messages about people who devote a great deal of energy to ensure that they can get back at, or get even with, their former friends, spouses, or enemies for perceived wrongs that have been done to them.

The Challenges

(And There Are Many)

Here's the problem. NONE OF US IS PERFECT! All right, you may be the one exception. Generally speaking, we are all perfectly imperfect. Do most people harm us intentionally? I don't think so. There are those who lack empathy, and there are sociopaths and psychopaths, many of whom are running large and successful corporations. They cannot understand why people feel victimized by them when they fire them, shut companies down to maximize profits, or make themselves the center of attention.

The tragedy in Lac-Mégantic, Quebec, was a telling example. Here, you had a CEO, a man who had reduced the train's crew down to one person, who had to do the jobs that several men had done in the past. One of their trains rolls into a town creates a burning inferno killing 47 men, women, and children and destroying the lives and homes of countless others. Then the CEO goes on national television in the US and Canada and complains that no one appreciates that he's come to Canada to see the damage for himself.

He cannot fathom the harm created or the tragic and negative consequences that his actions had by reducing the number of employees on a train. His goal was to maximize profits. In the years to come, the question that will be examined is, Was this an avoidable tragedy? And, he gets upset on national television because the people of the town are angry with him and then says, "I'm never coming back here again."

However, no one in town will ever find peace until they can forgive him. That doesn't mean he should get away with not accepting some responsibility for the events of that July night in 2013.

Nelson Mandela recognized the need for forgiveness and never looked back in anger at the men who had robbed him of the majority of his adult life. He came out of prison and led South Africa through arguably one of the most remarkable political transformations in history. There were no reprisal murders, no violence, and no widespread civil disobedience. And, did the white South African's go through a very challenging time? I suspect none of us who were there will ever know. But they did manage to transform the country peacefully. We must forgive everyone in our lives if we are truly to find happiness. Again, no one is immune from this basic human emotion. We all have it. I suspect even Mother Theresa had it at times.

What happens frequently is we are unable to forgive ourselves for things we've done in the past. This belief is a double-edged sword, too. It robs us of life's energy and joy. It is really important to recognize that we are worthy human beings. We all make mistakes. Some of us have done terrible things in the past. Others of us have just done the normal things — yelled at our children, gossiped about someone we didn't like, lied to someone, or stolen something when we were children. But, we feel we are the only ones who could have done anything this bad.

You may have cheated on your spouse. You may have cheated on your expense account at work. One of the great things about a Master Mind group is that we can befriend someone that we trust, share this information with them, and finally experience relief.

Possible Solutions

We may be Catholic or Anglican and turn to the sacrament of reconciliation. We can go to our minister or a friend and just acknowledge our wrongdoing. It is vital for peace of mind and healthy self-esteem to unburden ourselves of these typical flaws.

Is there anything new here I'm saying? Absolutely not! It's been known since the beginning of recorded history. In Matthew 18:21–22 when Peter asks Christ if he should forgive someone seven times, Christ responds not seven times but seventy-seven times.

In other words, forgiveness has to be

infinite. We must continue to forgive those who've harmed us because otherwise we allow anger and resentment go grow inside of us like a cancerous cell. It will eventually eat you alive and rob you of your peace of mind and true happiness. And the good news is that because we forgive, so we are forgiven.

How do we forgive, especially when we have really been betrayed? Perhaps our spouse has cheated on us, perhaps our friends have taken advantage of our generosity and then done something that has hurt us deeply. Perhaps we've loaned money to someone close to you, and they've not paid you back or taken responsibility for the loan.

Perhaps we've been lied about and hurt in business by someone we really trusted and thought was our friend. Any one of these events is enough to cause anyone of us a great deal of pain and suffering. Our instinct is to strike back in anger and get even. First we have to make sure that our faulty filter has not been at work. Here's the downside to anger and resentment. We only end up hurting ourselves when we stay angry with someone. In my opinion, here are the facts. No one gets away with anything in life. While certain people may enjoy a temporary benefit from taking advantage of us or hurting us, eventually, it comes back on the perpetrator. It may take some time, but, enviably, a price has to be paid by all of us for our deeds. By the way, this is true of positive behavior too. The South Asians call it the law of Karma. We in North America have a phrase: "What goes around comes around."

The fact is those who commit this offense eventually end up paying a price for it. No one gets away with anything in this life. Period! These are indisputable laws of nature. The universe is set up like this, in my opinion. Our species continue to try and circumvent these laws and time after time, we are taught lessons.

The same is true in our business dealings, which is why it is imperative for those in control of our economy to wake up. We can only go so long with a very small percentage of the population controlling the majority of the wealth. Greed really has taken over. It's not healthy for anyone with extreme wealth to hoard it. I am not a socialist either. I have always been and will always be a capitalist. But I know that when the balance goes out as it has now, we are on very dangerous ground. The whole economic system could very well collapse and put our society into a further recession unlike any we've ever seen before. It is not beyond the pale of possibility that this could be the catalyst for a revolution, the likes of which the United States has not seen since 1776. We need a healthy middle class to keep the machine functioning properly. It is not functioning at any level at this moment.

Can we consciously connect our behavior to past events? You can do a simple test in your life. Think of a time, when you have gossiped or said something about someone you didn't like or who had hurt you. Now, think about a time when some days, weeks, months, or years later, you found yourself on the receiving end of the same behavior. Think of a time when you've known someone who was doing something that you knew was immoral, or dishonest. At first it appears that they were getting away with it. Then what happens? They get caught and find themselves on the receiving end of similar actions. It is a closed loop. It is an energy source that must complete its cycle.

Right actions lead to right outcomes. The outcomes may not happen immediately, but they will if we keep working toward them. It is important for us to be proactive in resolving our differences with others. Practically speaking, what can we do? All right, let's say a good friend hurts us in business. Let's say this is a person who we have really bent over backwards to help. Then they end up not only lying about us, and they manage to really cripple us emotionally because we feel so hurt. Worse yet, they may end up running off with our sweetheart or our business. Initially, it won't be easy to forgive them, and we might say a prayer like, "Dear God, bless that black-hearted bastard Harry, because I can't."

It's a start. I'm not saying we have to have perfection; I'm suggesting what has been suggested before, "progress, not perfection." Conversely, if you have gossiped or cheated or stolen money from someone you may have to go to them and clean up your side of the street. This action is not an action to be taken lightly. And, this is exactly where a Master Mind group can support you in taking the correct action.

You may need to sit down and look at your

part in it. If you've been cheating on your best friend's wife or husband, I don't know that it is a good idea to go up and say to either spouse, "I've been sleeping with your wife/husband, and I'm sorry."

First, you are leading with your chin, and you may end up with a slap in the face, or worse, destroy a marriage. Did his wife ask you to do this? Seek guidance again from your Master Mind partners, as you don't want to bring harm to a third party.

You cannot seek your peace of mind at the expense of another. It may be appropriate to declare to your Master Mind partners, "I have been doing this behavior. I request that all of you pray for me to get the spiritual guidance and help I need to stop."

You may have harmed someone in business. You may have gossiped or lied about someone or spread false rumors about their integrity when you were angry with them.

With the guidance of your Master Mind partners, you may set up a time to visit the person you've harmed. Regardless of what flaws they have you are not there to discuss their weaknesses or personality traits. You are there to clean up your part in whatever situation has arisen. Often when we do this, amazing things happen. People are overwhelmed by our honesty and forthright admission, and we see a healing take place right in front of our eyes.

And Now, Let's Talk About Death!

Just in case you were starting to feel too good, I thought I should bring a little reality into the discussion to keep us all stabilized. When I was a young man in the insurance business, I noticed that when I said to a young woman "It's no joke to croak if you are broke," she would just head for the hills or the nearest exit. There's not a lot we can say humorously about this subject except what Woody Allen has said. We do need to look at the importance of cleaning up our relationships with our family or close friends before we die. How many of us will leave this planet with unresolved differences with our immediate family members? I suspect some us will.

Whether we are talking about brothers and sisters or sons and daughters or in-laws or extended family or ex-husbands or wives, it would be in all of our best interests to clean up these relationships. We've all had disagreements with our siblings, or children, parents, or friends. But is that how you want to be remembered? I don't. In my case, I had to make amends to my oldest children from my first marriage. I'd moved out to Vancouver to attend university and stayed for 12 years. As a result, I didn't participate in their upbringing. I was an absent father. It took a significant amount of time, and the willingness to keep reaching out. To my children's credit, they were very gracious in their forgiveness of me. But it took time.

When I was young, I used to apologize for getting up in the morning. I was always sorry. It was a constant state. As I matured, people didn't want to hear how sorry I was, they wanted to see action. When I lost a great deal of money in 1986, I couldn't stand saying I was sorry any longer for the movie I'd produced that was an unmitigated disaster both creatively and financially. It should never have been produced. I made the decision to move ahead without the funds in place.

At first I was cavalier about it. I just assumed that I'd always be able to find a solution as I had in the past and clean up the mess and this time would be no different.

However, this time we were on the receiving end of rather unscrupulous individuals who saw us coming a mile away. If you saw the movie *The*

Sting ... well, we got stung. After paying a lawyer in New York City, he kept reassuring us we could begin production. We hired a crew of over 100 people. We began production. The promised money we paid for never materialized and thus begun the most dramatic, debilitating period of my life. It's taken me over 25 years to clean up that wreckage from my past. There were people who really did hope I would find myself shuffling off my mortal coil sooner than later and meeting the source of all evil in a very fiery pit of hot, burning coals, fire, and whatever horrible suffering I would endure.

In retrospect, I can't say I blame them. In truth, I've reached out to as many of them as I can and wherever possible I've tried to make personal or financial amends. And I learned to forgive the offending lawyer for being less than forthright.

Here's what is interesting about that

experience. I've never done it again. Even though I continue to be in the midst of a very trying time as a result of my brain injury, I am extremely proactive in reaching out to my creditors and shareholders. I am letting them know where I am and what I am doing. There is one with whom my contact is minimal.

Equally important is the fact that I pray every day that if there is anyone I have hurt financially, spiritually, or emotionally that they can forgive me. I did a lot of crazy things when I was a young man. Things I can't even imagine doing today. But, I know I've hurt people — not intentionally, but through my misguided behavior that was the result of the trauma of my childhood.

What I've tried to do is give people the space to be able to tell me just how angry they are or how hurt they were. And I'm very clear about boundaries. I have no issue with anyone saying, "I think you were a selfish, self-centered jerk" (or expletive), and they can say it once. But there is no room for abuse. Saying it once is enough. What I tell them ahead of meeting them is if they wish to be abusive, or in any way violent, that is where I draw the line. I don't do abuse. And there is a significant difference between an honest communication and abusive behavior.

I find that when I am cleaning up relationships it is very important to let the person know, "I hear how angry you are. I can see that I've hurt you a great deal. I am truly sorry for that, and I'm willing to repair our relationship by going to any lengths, including never contacting you again if that is what you want." For some people, that may be the kindest thing we can do because seeing us just brings up too many painful memories for them. In my case, that's not been the outcome. In some cases, such as my dad's, I had to go to his grave. My father hurt me a great deal as a child. I don't need to go into the specifics here, but it traumatized me, and left me incredibly damaged and has taken a lifetime to heal.

What I did is I visited the town where he was born and is buried. I stood at his grave and told him how much pain he had caused me and then I told him I forgave him and wished his soul peace and acceptance. I now realize just how troubled he was, dying alone, with none of us around him. We reap what we sow.

A great deal of emotion washed over me, and I just stood there as tears flowed down my face. At last I could let my dad go. I told him I loved him, and I'm sure he loved me too, even though he never uttered those words to me as a child. When I'm speaking or teaching in my class, I often say, "It's incredible how hard I am on myself. If anyone ever did to me what I do to myself, I'd charge him or her with assault and battery."

So many of us are just so hard on ourselves. It is really important to learn to forgive ourselves and just learn to lighten up and accept ourselves, warts and all. If people would be totally honest, even those who seem to have exemplary lives will admit that they often berate themselves for simple mistakes. We all need forgiveness. It's imperative for our mental well-being.

.

Chapter Ten

I Ask

STEP 6. I ASK

I make known my specific requests, asking my partner's support in knowing that the Master Mind is fulfilling my needs. (Make your request now: "I request ____.")

GROUP RESPONSE: *"I know the Master Mind has heard you and is providing you with what you have asked for."*

Talk about one of the most confusing parts of this whole process. One of my big problems is that my mind (faulty filter) starts chatting to me around five in the morning when I come to after a night's sleep. In my mind and sitting on the end of my bed is the little guy whom I mentioned earlier and who resides in my head, and he just smiles at me with that "Oh, I know something you don't!" Then he starts up, "It's not okay to ask

God for something because you don't deserve it. How selfish can you be when millions are starving to death? You know money is the root of all evil!"

Those thoughts spin endlessly in a repetitive loop like a rotisserie in my mind. They are interspersed with "You are not worthy. Who do you think you are? What a lot of nonsense. Do you think God is up there like a short-order cook waiting to fill your order?" Then my inner voice kicks in and responds to the previous thoughts, "I don't know, maybe?"

However, when we look at scripture there is a lot of "Ask and you will receive, seek and you will find, knock and it will be opened to you." On that theme, as far as money being evil, it's inanimate. It is just something we exchange for goods and services. The "love of money is the root of all evil." When I sell out my integrity, be blatantly dishonest, or just enrich myself at the expense of someone else, I am headed for big trouble.

I have been in three Master Mind groups over the past 15 years. My first one ended when I left Toronto and moved to Eastern Ontario in 2001. When my second Master Mind group began, I was in the business of just asking for financial help. Over a period of years, we had a lawyer, a former member of the Royal Canadian Mounted Police and then a former military officer. That group eventually came down to just three of us. Richard, Bill, who was an avowed agnostic and retired psychiatrist, and myself. The three of us held over 600 meetings over a six- or seven-year period. It was Bill who got us to start to examine the concept of asking for humility and clarity of thought.

At first my mind railed against this idea. I kept asking for financial help. With Bill's influence I began to shift my emphasis and ask for help with my business, my finances, my relationship with my then wife Deb, and my children Brendan and Laurel (who were teenagers at the time). I also asked for a healing with my children from my first marriage, Andrew and Colleen. Slowly I began to come around to Bill's way of thinking. I can remember saying for the first time, "Okay, please guide me to peace of mind and humility."

I was expecting that I would have to drop to my knees right there in the restaurant or join the Salvation Army, which I actually have tremendous respect for and acknowledge that as an organization on the front lines of those in need is arguably one of the most loving and respectful. I saw humility — let me correct that statement — I perceived humility as a fatal flaw, a weakness. Once again, here I was at the mercy of my faulty filter and misinformation from my childhood.

I never recognized that humility was something worth pursuing in itself. I never imagined it could be the key to true happiness and serenity. I'm not suggesting for one moment that I have it, but today. I see the value in seeking it, as it provides so many benefits when I choose to ask for it in my everyday life.

Many of us hold the attitude that people would walk all over us if we were humble. We confuse humility with humiliation. I know the difference from the perspective of syntax and semantics, but not in terms of emotions.

Still, when I looked around, whom did I admire? My friend Bill for one! In spite of his extensive medical knowledge, and his numerous degrees that included a specialty in anesthesiology, he never talked about his training or made a big deal of it. He was just a very, very humble man. I came to have a tremendous amount of love and respect for him. My friend Richard was the same way. In fact, most of the people I like and admire are exactly the same way. If anyone were the odd man out, it was me when I think about it.

Learning what to ask and pray for was a big part of the journey for many of us. Getting through the thought that we are worthy of any Higher Power or God's love was also another hurdle, which many of us had to overcome. It is amazing to me how many of us have been so dramatically affected by our upbringings. Not that anyone recognized or acknowledged it back then. It's just the way things were, especially if you were to view my family from the outside. We lived in a very beautiful home, and my father had been a civic politician and a successful insurance executive. It didn't fit the picture of what people thought of alcoholism and violence back in those days.

Coming to a place of acceptance that there was a Power in the first place (that was not like my father), then accepting the idea that this

Power could be personal to me and that this same Higher Power could and would help me if I asked Him/Her/It too, was a very radical idea. As I said earlier, if you already have a traditional faith, you are that much further ahead of where I am. I began with very simple requests. "Can I receive $1 million or $2 million?" That didn't work too well. "Can you please guide me to the best possible result with my creditors?" That worked. "Can you please guide me to the best possible result with a project, so the greatest good is produced for all involved?" That worked. "Can you please guide me to financial solvency?" That worked. "Can you please guide me to peace of mind, humility, and clarity of thought?" Wow, that started to kick in.

Then slowly I began to see and understand that there were many areas of my life where I needed guidance. I was dumbfounded by the turn of events between the time I was whereby not one of the 312 projects we pitched had been approved.

You see, there I was thinking, "Okay, I can control this. I can fix this if I just put my mind to it." No, I can't!

Acceptance of this fact was the beginning of understanding that the brain injury had hurt me in ways I couldn't have comprehended. I kept thinking that I had always been able to overcome every obstacle in my past, so surely I could overcome this! It was this specific discovery that drove me to begin the process of surrendering. After 46 years of seeking a spiritual practice, I was still trying to run the show myself.

As far as my spiritual life was concerned, I was now willing to turn it over. When it came to my career, money, or romantic relationships, hold on there God, I can handle those. If you can only please guide me to the success I've been asking for, all will be well.

In retrospect, if I had kept going I would

have continued to see the same results. All I would have ended up doing was wasting the money I had in reserve while trying to get yet another production going. When I earnestly began to seek a Higher Power's guidance, it started to produce results. Big results like the overwhelming "NO!"

That was difficult to comprehend. I have or had a very simplistic view of God. In fact, it was very immature. I know that Scripture also talks about having the faith of a child. I had the magical thinking of a child. Apparently Steve Jobs had it too, and it essentially killed him because he thought he could overcome his cancer through very basic and childlike beliefs — just meditate, eat vegan, stay away from meat.

Not one of those things in themselves is bad, though, in my opinion, they are not a replacement for science or modern medicine. In retrospect, he would have been better served with a combination of both disciplines.

In my case, I have to let go of this kind of thinking that just because I'm doing everything correctly, the results are always going to go my way. If I'm seeking spiritual guidance, I have to be ready to accept "no" as an answer also. Perhaps a better prayer is "Thy will be done."

The interesting thing is that when I did the Canfield Coaching, I came to realize that I had an incredible number of things to work out. Far more yeses than nos.

I've not been exactly hard done by. It was only through looking at my life with a new lens that I began to see all the wonderful accomplishments I've been able to achieve. For example, being an award-winning professor is almost enough for the average person to feel good about themselves. Include all of the film and television I've produced and that would be more than enough for the average human being.

Add to that working with amazing people Like John Munro and Vicki Keith (the world record holder in marathon swimming) in assisting them to make *Penguins Can Fly*, a film about children with special needs, and that would be enough. The film played in Los Angeles for Academy Award consideration and helped raise a significant amount of money for the various YMCAs that have programs for kids with both physical and intellectual disabilities.

Plus, it has been an incredible privilege to be the author of this book. I've had the pleasure of speaking to a significant number of people over the years about overcoming adversity. All these events have been extremely positive and have led to a real sense of gratitude and accomplishment.

As a result of this realization, I've come to another conclusion. I don't know what is good for me or anyone else a great deal of the time. My mind says, "Of course you know." But I don't.

Letting Go and Letting the Master Mind

What I was learning through the process of letting go of my business and possibly my career was that there may be something I was better suited for as a career. As discussed above, I looked into the possibilities of teaching and writing non-fiction books as well as inspirational and motivational speaking. I could even continue to pursue writing and producing film and television. Or, maybe it would be a combination of all of the above. As they say, "When one door closes, another opens."

What can I ask my Master Mind Partners for? Anything I want. With this caveat: "If what I have asked for is not what is best for me, please send me what I need instead of what I want."

Having goals as well as having a plan for your life and, asking for guidance, is paramount to finding your heart's desire.

I've known all my life that I want to share

with others what I've learned along the way. But, I was such a nonconformist in my earlier years that my mind (faulty filter) still says, "Dave, you are too much of a rebel for mainstream society to embrace." In fact, I've discovered that I am incredibly conservative with liberal leanings.

I am so grateful to say that during the three weeks involved in deciding to move to Vancouver I felt a conscious contact with The Divine that I've never felt before. Getting here to West Vancouver fulfills a dream I've had for years. I had a vision of an apartment with a view of what I was looking for; only it was up a little higher up the mountain. Then I made the decision that if I move here, I want to be closer to the two small towns that make up West Vancouver, Ambleside, and Dundarave. I want to ride my bike and go for walks and not have to get in my car all the time. I'm finally getting sick of driving to go anywhere. One of the downsides of living in the country is you have to drive everywhere.

I did ask for guidance about seeking this teaching job at the university, about selling my house, moving out of two places with only five days' notice. The fact that I was able to deal with my Toronto apartment and rent out my house in the country was a miracle in itself. I'm astounded at how it all just came together with so many kind people pitching in to give me a hand.

Admittedly, one of the most difficult things for me to do is ask anyone for help. I am always happy to help others if I can, but there is some quirk in me that I struggle with when asking others for the same. It's not healthy for them or me, as I rob people of the opportunity to feel good by being able to be of service.

I did originally ask the Master Mind for help. To keep my production company functioning, I worked as hard as I ever had in my entire career. I don't know how I could have worked any harder, smarter, or more diligently. In the end, I was left with either gaining acceptance of the result or getting angry and resentful.

I had to accept that I have an injury. Mine is a very specific injury that affects my selling ability. I seem to be okay writing this as I'm relating to my experience. This I can do. And it is very therapeutic writing it. So, there is a very specific emotional benefit to it.

No Is Also an Answer

"We don't always get what we ask for" is another lesson I've learned, as well as "No is also an answer." It may be that I can't see why it would be "no" at the time. Or it might seem grossly unfair to me. But if I look back on my life and honestly examine the result of some of the most difficult periods I've ever had, then I see why in retrospect I had to feel that disappointment. As I said before, I've never learned anything on a good day.

Yes Does Happen Too

Yes does happen too. I did ask for a teaching position, and it did come up almost miraculously. I did ask to live where I am right now. And they're both literally what I had hoped for. You could never have predicted either one of those outcomes a short while ago. All of the shows that we did produce were stellar in both their ratings and creativity. I've been praying for a deeper, more meaningful relationship with the Higher Power of my understanding. That seems to be manifesting. I've also asked my Master Mind group to help me achieve my written goals and find peace of mind and humility. And, now I find myself working away on a beautiful sunny and warm Friday afternoon in West Vancouver.

I'm asking The Master Mind to guide me to the best possible outcomes and to the best results I can produce today in every area of my life. Only time will tell if these results match my other ones.

However, I don't suggest going out and nearly getting beaten to death like I did to discover a new way to live. There are smarter ways to do this, but it appears that this experience was to be part of my journey.

I've asked two of my friends about forming a Master Mind group here. It has already been eight weeks since I left Ontario, and the only thing I miss besides my children and friends are my Master Mind connections. I've phoned both Richard and Bruce on a few occasions and spoken to Will once. I'm keeping the connections alive.

I am also praying more now than I ever have, and I am sincerely seeking guidance. My friend and accountant out here, Mike, whom I've known for over 30 years has given me a series of Unity lectures that I'm finding very helpful. One thing about being on my own much of the time is I have a lot of time to meditate and think about life. I've done all those things in spades recently.

It is important for me, or anyone else, to have the support of fellow travelers. The question I would ask myself is, If I had to leave the planet tonight, would I be satisfied with my life so far? My answer is that I would be grateful for all the blessings I've had. Has my life been perfect? No, but, it's been very, very good, and I've been very blessed.

I am human and thus imperfect, so my mind quickly forgets all that when I don't get what I want. Have I mentioned my chronic infantile omnipotence? My late friend Jack Humphrey gave me that expression, and I love it. That's when you don't get what you want and you lay on the floor and flail away. Acceptable at the age of one, irritating at the age of two, downright rude as a young man or woman, and just plain embarrassing as an adult. But guess what? I still get bouts of it. I just mask it better.

I think if we keep asking for guidance and have a sincere desire in our hearts to change and be of service, then I suspect we will find ourselves in a much better place than if it is only material possessions we seek.

I don't necessarily want to downplay material achievements either. I would still like to be financially self-supporting and able to live a comfortable lifestyle. At some point, I would like to be able to spend a few months per year in a warm climate during the worst of the rainy season here. I would still like to continue to have nice cars and money to maintain them. I want to be able to eat healthily and buy the nutritious food and vitamins that I need to maintain my health. I want to continue to belong to the West Vancouver Fitness and Aquatic Center where I was this morning. I want to be able to go out once a week to a show or a movie and have dinner out a few nights a week. If I am fortunate enough to meet someone wonderful, I would always like to be able to enjoy treating her to a nice holiday or a road trip.

One of the things I did today was to examine my finances. I spoke to the payroll department of the university, where I'm teaching. I am only teaching 10 hours per week, and I now know what my net income per month will be for the next four months (the length of my contract). I have no guarantee that the contract will be renewed. I will have to cash in some of my retirement investments unless my house sells. I have asked the Divine Intelligence to guide me to my greatest good in this area, and I will call Richard and Bruce to ask them if they can pray for me too. I will arrange to meet with my accountant Mike and perhaps one other friend, and do a review of what my options are. Some business guidance would be helpful.

While I feel nervous about it, I'm not feeling

panicked. I do think that I'm going to be guided to the best outcome. I've been marking the first 50 or 60 papers for my new students. I have my lecture prepared for Wednesday and Thursday of this week. I'm ahead of the curve on being organized. The critical thing is that these four months are giving me the chance to take stock of my life and reprioritize what it is that I want to do. I can then create a plan to achieve those goals.

I've responded to one of the insurance companies that is handling my disability claim. I have followed through with some calls and emails. This morning I prayed and asked to be the most productive that I can be. I've broken my day down into manageable chunks. I don't have to take on all my issues at once. As an example, last Friday I wrote to the president of Wells Fargo Bank in San Francisco. No one in the bank has any experience with someone like me coming to them ahead of every default and asking them to stop payments and interest while I resolve my pending legal case.

All I can do is be rigorously honest with them. I sent the proposal and letter out to them a few weeks ago, and I have not heard anything back yet. I will let you know how it goes. After all, he is the president of one the largest banks in the United States, dealing in billions of dollars. I'm sure he's got a few more important things on his plate than Dave Brady's letter about a modest line of credit. It turns out I've paid about 125% of what I had originally borrowed in interest payments alone over the past four years because I've been fundamentally unconscious about these matters since my injury.

October 4, 2013

I've spoken to the executive office at Wells Fargo, and it would appear they're not able to do anything for me. I've asked the young man I spoke to if he could speak to someone on my behalf at an executive level.

None of the folks I'm talking to have any authority to make an actual decision except to say "no."

From a corporate communications point of view, it is interesting to see how different corporate cultures function. Two years ago I had a problem with a major airlines. They wouldn't allow us to take all of our gear on one flight as it was in the Rocky Mountains in Colorado. I was flying my crew to location for the *Doc Zone* filming of "Super Volcano, Yellowstone's Fury" and I had contacted the president's office to discuss the problem with him. Not only did he respond within a day, but also on the day he called his staff cleared up the problem for me. Today I share that positive story with as many people as I can. There is no doubt in my mind about the success of this airline and why I am one of their Gold Members. What a powerful example the CEO was. He genuinely seems to care. I'd like to hope that John Stumpf is the same kind of person.

It wasn't for some time, that I received a very nice letter from Wells Fargo Bank. The bank has declined my request to put my payments on hold while I resolve my financial issues with the insurance company. I don't believe the CEO was ever made aware of my situation. I did propose that the bank look at purchasing bulk copies of this book upon its publication, and I would be happy to come down and speak to some of their clients on the challenges associated with aging and overcoming adversity. They acknowledged that all my payments were up to date.

The bank did express interest in receiving a copy of my book. I am grateful that this could keep the door open and at some point I hope to speak to the CEO in person, at which point I will mention this experience to him. I looked him up online and see, that like me, he grew up in the northern US, near the border with Canada, and seems like a very decent guy.

One of the challenges I've always had is that I want things NOW. If I pray and ask my Master Mind group for something today, I'm hoping I'll have the answer tomorrow, or the next day, at the latest.

If I could speak to God in person, I'd have to say, "What's with your timeline? Boy, you can be slow." Okay, there are 7.1 billion people all pleading, crying, and asking for help. "Help me, guide me, save me, save this member of my family." "Heal whoever, get that rotten bastard over there — oops." I say this remembering that, as the banker, God may be a tad busy. I'm not actually sure that God Himself/Herself/Itself actually sits around figuring out who to save, fix, heal, reward, punish, chastise, pat on the back, or kick in the ass. We do have free will. The point is I think most of us do a very good job of doing all those nasty things to ourselves. I suspect poor old God just sits there in a state of amazement at how hard we are on ourselves and one another.

As we strive to grow in humility and acquire a conscious contact through prayer and meditation, we're led to the understanding that we can access the Divine Spark, which is the living presence of the Divine Intelligence within us. Or, we have within us the power that has emerged from the universe since its inception, that is, the consciousness of this Power. And that is what many of us are coming to believe. We all have within us this Divine Spark that if we are attuned to Divine Grace, we can find solutions that would baffle others. We can deal with pain and calamity in a way that others are not able to. We can enjoy life and feel good about all of our experiences, both positive and negative, and we see the real value in experiencing them as a necessary part of our growth.

It is important to keep asking our Master Mind partners for guidance until we know that we have the right answer. Once again, we may have to pray for acceptance of the way things are. Especially if what we've asked for does not appear.

I just glanced out the window and the late afternoon sun is highlighting the clouds over Vancouver Island, and there are no words to describe just how beautiful it is, cloudy or not. There are about a half dozen large ocean-going container ships anchored in the harbor off Point Grey. Thank you, God, for the beauty of this world.

The Greatest Answered Prayer of My Life

I want to end this chapter with perhaps the most important prayer I ever uttered in my entire life, outside of the day in New York City when I got down on my knees in Saint Patrick's Cathedral and asked, "If there is a God, please help me." At that moment, all of my cravings for mood-altering substances were removed from my life and have never returned. It occurred the day my youngest daughter Laurel was born.

Laurel weighed only 880 grams (less than two pounds) when she was born and was probably one of the youngest premature babies ever to survive; her little torso fit in the palm of my hand, where she slept for the first three nights of her life because I didn't want to let go of her. I remember going into a bathroom at St. Joseph's Hospital in London, Ontario, getting down on my knees, and sobbing uncontrollably, begging God to spare her. My mother, who had been at Sick Children's Hospital for the latter part of her nursing career, had told me not to get my hopes up.

The doctors warned us of the potential

pitfalls that lay ahead as they had no experience with such a small baby in 1989. Laurel's bilirubin was so high they had to exchange all of her blood within 48 hours of her birth. She was intubated, and they warned us that because her lungs had not matured that there could be ventricle hemorrhaging (brain bleeding). That procedure could cause unknown learning disabilities or the potential loss or impairment of her eyesight, as well as other physical maladies. Then we had to cope with her heart stopping randomly over the first few weeks of her life. She was having cardiac events called bradycardias, where her heart would stop, and we would have to take her little feet and tickle them so her heart would start up again. She had so many tubes in her; it was just so painful to watch it all unfolding.

When I think back now and look at Laurel today, beautiful, incredibly intelligent, the most amazing blue eyes you've ever seen, a real fighter who is just such a remarkable young woman, I am filled with gratitude. In spite of the doctors' dire warnings, she has successfully completed her university degree with honors, has just received her first paying position as a speaker, and has already launched a new play she's written and will star in, with her brother Brendan directing. I'm amazed. That ask was perhaps the most important prayer of my life, and I am so grateful that it was answered in the affirmative, I probably should not complain ever again if not another request is answered.

Chapter Eleven

I Give Thanks

STEP 7. I GIVE THANKS

I give thanks that the Master Mind is responding to my needs and I assume the same feelings I would have if my requests were fulfilled.

It is a well-known fact that our minds cannot differentiate between the perceived and the actual circumstances in our lives. In other words, if we speak out loud and affirm, "I am grateful today that the Master Mind is guiding me to peace of mind, prosperity, real joy in my life and the best possible outcome in all my affairs," our Master Mind begins to work to bring about the very results that we are giving thanks for. If we want more in our life, we give thanks for what we have. When I was in the thick of my recent challenges, what did I do? I had to pray and meditate to ensure that I didn't focus on what I wasn't getting. When I did break down and worry, which I did from time to time because none of us is perfect, I was praying for what I didn't want. I'm not talking about healthy caution and concern about our well-being. What I'm talking about is repetitive, compulsive worry; the worrying that robs us of peace of mind and harms the relationships we have with those closest to us. When we give thanks for the simple things in life, we open the floodgate of blessings. We begin attracting to us those things we desire to have. If we have good health, we give thanks.

Earlier I mentioned having a gratitude list. I have a gratitude list in the front of my daily journal, which I read every morning. Included in it are my children, my brothers and sisters, my nieces and nephews. I also include my past career successes; my nice new apartment in West Vancouver; my new teaching position; my friends, all the good things I have in my life now, and all I have been given. This gratitude keeps me in a state of Grace.

When we begin giving thanks for the entire blessing we've been given, and when we share with others what we have been given, we also open ourselves up for a lot of good to come into our lives. There is an old saying, "If you want to keep what you have, give it away."

In other words, if something is working for you and you feel a real sense of gratitude for it, share it with others. It can be as simple as swimming two or three days a week, and then telling others you care about how good you feel and the obvious physical benefits of exercise. It won't matter if they take you up on your offer to swim with them. Just trying to be of service opens you up for more benefits.

Tithing is the same way with respect to money, and it is something I now try to do, even when I'm worried about money. I am tithing 10% of everything I get and, believe me, I never seem to miss it, as it seems always to be replaced by something of equal or greater value.

When we make the decision to imagine how we would feel if we received what our heart's desire is, then we open up a magical channel straight to the source of all things in the universe. It's why creative people and inventors can step out in faith and have amazing results come to pass in their lives. They experience the very thing we're examining here. On many occasions, they will often appear to have failed, but to these remarkable individuals, it is just a temporary setback. Thomas Edison said, "I have not failed. I've just found 10,000 ways that won't work."
Once again the New Testament provides us with evidence from the Gospels, and I'm sure there will also be a similar writing in the Torah or other religious texts. In Mark 11:22–24 it reads,

"Whatever you ask in prayer, believe that you have received it, and it will be done for you."

Now I suspect there must be some common-sense caveats attached to this. One, you must believe in something greater than yourself. Two, you can't be asking for anything that would harm anyone. Three, you can't have "wrong motives." You can't be asking to have a buddy down the road drop dead because you covet his wife. Or, if you are that buddy's wife, you can't be coveting Fred next door because he's more successful than your husband.

The point is that if we have a strong belief in a Power greater than ourselves, if we practice prayer and meditation, and if we are truly seeking to increase our awareness of the Master Mind's will in our lives and we want to be of service to others, then we will increase our chances exponentially of attracting to us what we really desire.

The great thing too about having a Master Mind group is that we have a sounding board for many of our requests. It also helps us in the process of coming to believe that our requests are being answered.

Affirmations work. It is an interesting experiment to step out in faith and believe that you already possess what you want. There is a law of attraction, and this is one of the keys to it. That is why both the book and film, *The Secret*, were so successful.

There are numerous books on success principles, including Jack Canfield's, which is just an extrapolation on the work of Napoleon Hill. However, all books, including the wonderful book by Catherine Ponder, *Open Your Mind to Prosperity*, say the same thing.

It does work if we allow ourselves to reinforce our belief by affirming "I am receiving," and then add what it is you wish to attain. If we affirm it out loud, we can often feel a chill go through us, which seems to be a sort of conscious contact with the "source" of all abundance, peace, and knowledge.

How do we know if the Master Mind is responding to our needs? Often, as was the case of my recent university appointment, the thought popped into my head in the process of meditating to check that specific university to see if it had any teaching assignments listed.

I had mentioned to my Master Mind group that I needed a change. Something had to give as I'd gone through the previously mentioned 300 "nos" on my new film and television projects.

It was effortless. When I looked online that day, I saw the advertisement for the position. I had less than 48 hours in which to submit my application.

Prior to that, I was praying, writing, and just hammering as hard as I could to close a deal.

I was so focused on closing and creating new projects that I couldn't see that the answer over and over was "no." I was on the verge of causing myself serious physical harm with stress and worry because of the incessant number of "nos" I was receiving.

It was also beginning to affect my self-esteem. I was not feeling good about myself. I was grappling emotionally trying to accept that what I had in the past was gone — as far as some of my creative gifts were concerned. I also didn't know if this injury was going to leave me permanently disabled, or if it was something temporary.

However, I didn't stop asking for guidance and help. I've never really been able to accept defeat in the past. Especially, in this case, as I had to give up a business that I had only started up four years before. Prior to this unfortunate event, we were headed on a straight trajectory toward all the success I'd ever hoped for in my career.

Unanswered Prayer

This raises one of the questions that has plagued me my entire life. If God or the Master Mind does hear us, why does He/She/It not answer all prayers? How do we explain the horrors of Lac-Mégantic, the tsunami in Asia,, or the World Trade Center? Did many of them not pray and believe they would be helped?

This is the paradox of faith. I admit that I have a limited understanding of the universe. I don't know what the Master Mind's will is for any of us as I indicated earlier. It is impossible to know why these events seem to occur randomly and are beyond our comprehension. What is also inconceivable is why any of us must sometimes suffer so much pain and horror before death. It doesn't make any sense at all from a logical point of view.

I know that we all have to face death, and for many of us it will be sooner rather than later. That raises many questions: What does lie on the other side? What is the point of suffering with terminal illness? Why do people suffer so much in this life? Why do innocent people die in tragic accidents? I don't know. I don't. This was the argument posed by British atheist Christopher Hitchens in his book *God Is Not Great*. His case intrigued me. Here was a man who was clearly way smarter than I was. Nonetheless, I started to dig into his story. I would discover that according to certain reports, he died an active alcoholic and that according to rumor from people close to the family his mother had committed suicide after having an affair with a Church of England minister.

Suddenly I can see why he would have the feeling that God is not great! He was such a brilliant writer and an incredibly dedicated human being. I would have enjoyed speaking with him. When I was a young man and working with some left-leaning folks, I too was an avowed agnostic. I could never have the absolute faith of an atheist. Now I have seen evidence, irrefutable evidence, that when we do pray and ask for guidance and help we get it.

Master Mind Groups

Many of us may have had Master Mind groups without knowing it if we were involved in any kind of spiritual or philosophical movements. There were also the human potential movements of the 1970s, such as EST (Erhard Seminars Training), of which I was a big fan. I did the training, the seven-day, the workshops and, in essence, many of these seminars and workshops would set up the dynamic that would further inspire me to pursue what I've come to know today as the Master Mind movement.

Is it new? Not really. It was Christ who said,

"For where two or three gather in my name, there am I with them." The Master Mind or Divine Intelligence is there and available to all of us if we just ask. There seems to be some Universal Intelligence, Divine Spirit, and undeniable force at work throughout the universe so that when we ask for help, we seem to get it.

For many, it is God who is the Master Mind. I'm more inclined to accept the concept of Mother/Father God or the Holy Spirit. I'm also not too worried whether or not He/She/It is going to fry my derrière when I get to the other side because I had doubts. And if you are one of the ones who think I am, then I humbly ask you to pray for me. Only time will tell which one of us is correct. I'm willing to bet my life on it; I've already been to hell. It holds no sway over me. As the old saying goes, "Religion is for those afraid of going to hell; spirituality, which I am an advocate of, is for those of us who've already been there." The

Master Mind likes me just as I am. So, I will continue to look at my list and continue to add to it.

The Lesson

In spite of my difficulties, I did give thanks. I did imagine myself sitting in this very chair writing, looking at the view that I am currently enjoying.

I do believe my life is taking a turn for the better. I will be able to get this book published. It will open doors for me to be of service through seminars and online webinars where I can personally share my journey with you.

If I can overcome a debilitating brain injury, shut down my company, let go of old ideas about others and myself and about notions of what success are, and just be grateful for what I have today, I am going to be all right.

Chapter Twelve

I Dedicate My Life

STEP 8. I DEDICATE MY LIFE

I now have a covenant in which it is agreed that the Master Mind is supplying me with an abundance of all things necessary to live a successful and happy life.

I dedicate myself to be of maximum service to God and those around me, to live in a manner that sets the highest example for others to follow; and to remain responsive to God's guidance.

I go forth with a spirit of enthusiasm, excitement, and expectancy. I am at peace.

As I sit here, the sky is almost mystical. I've never seen anything like it. The clouds are hanging layer upon layer over Point Grey, and the setting sun is reflecting off of them. They are a wonderful shade of gray and white with a tinge of pink. It was supposed to be raining today and instead it has turned into a gorgeous first day of fall. At this stage of my life, I no longer find myself limited to any specific theology or traditional formal religion. Although I may in the future. I've recently returned to two non-denominational Christian churches. One is called the Sutherland Church in North Vancouver where the minister there is Todd Weibe. He is a very unusual and bright young man who has an incredibly open mind. I'm glad I've met him and his friends. The other is the Unity Spiritual Center in Vancouver. I am very comfortable at both of them.

I sincerely believe that all these churches and faiths contain the answer to the big questions about faith and what it is we should be seeking in our lives. They also help me connect with a community of like-minded people. The older I get, the more I see how important this is for our emotional and spiritual well-being.

Michael Dowd's book *Thank God For Evolution* allows us to see just how it is that we all got to where we are and why. For so many of us, we are plagued by feelings of guilt, shame, blame, and a sense of failure as we look back on our lives. There is no need to be.

As stated in the opening, the purpose of this book is to guide you through the process of getting the most you can out of either your middle age or, as they euphemistically call it, your "golden years." Your goal should also be to find real peace of mind, happiness, and prosperity, regardless of your current circumstances. Your life can't be that much more precarious than mine is at the moment, unless, and heaven forbid, you've been diagnosed with a terminal illness. I can't compete with that. You may be one of those blessed people whose financial lives are on a rock-solid foundation, thus removing one of the greatest stressors in life. However, you may be one of those aching inside trying to understand how it is you got to this point having done everything right, but your life feels so wrong or incomplete.

I've spent the first two-thirds of my life *getting*. I would like to spend the last one-third *giving*. As the Good Book says, and I paraphrase, "It is better to give than to receive."

I have devoted much of my life to the pursuit of spiritual principles. Here is what I believe today. There is a God and it's not me. I like to think of Mother/Father God.

On a practical level, how can we utilize this step in our daily lives? As an example, I called my insurance company today to report my cracked windshield, which was damaged on the drive to Vancouver from Toronto. The insurance company has arranged for me to take my car into a garage tomorrow to get it replaced.

However, I have a Mercedes B200 Turbo. So the first challenge with this car is that the windshield will be one of three versions. One is standard glass, one is for automatic rain sensors, and the third is both rain-sensitive and light-sensitive. I found out I have the second type and it covered by my insurance. I am very grateful for this coverage, which has zero deductible.

My next challenge is that my Turbo Charger is not working properly. These can be very expensive parts or systems to repair, so I asked some friends about it. They gave me the name of a good Mercedes mechanic in Vancouver located under the Oak Street Bridge, who can hopefully repair the turbocharger.

Then everything in my life will be repaired. I just ask and believe that I am being supplied even at this mundane level of having to get my car fixed and that I'm guided to the right people. Let's see what happens.

How to Tell if Your Life Is Working

If you want to get a sense of how your life is working, glance around and see how many things need to be repaired in your life. How are your shoes? What is the condition of your home? Is it neat and tidy or filled with garbage or cluttered?

The Spirit of Enthusiasm Is Alive and Well

Well, here it is Tuesday, September 24th. I've come back from my new mechanic's, and he was kind enough to arrange for a rental car for me. Hans is German and has worked on Mercedes Benz's since 1965. I like that. He's one of us — a "boomer." What is interesting is how people, unrelated to him, were so quick to give him a wonderful endorsement as someone who was honest and did great work.

I also received word today from one of the major insurance companies that two of my claims have been approved because I have stopped working as the creator of television shows and movies. So far, so good! This covenant seems to be working.

Last week I did an online seminar with a young man in the United States, Steve Harrison. His focus is on the world of book publicity and marketing. He has helped a great number of best-selling authors get publicity for their books. As I suspected, he also pointed out that the best area to focus on to be of maximum service is to offer seminars, workshops, and weekend training sessions.

I now have confirmation that I'm headed in the right direction. I want to transform my life, let go of worry, and either heal from my physical disability or find a new way to compensate for it. I am grateful for my automobile insurance company, TD Meloche Monnex. They are amazing because they really care. I am also very grateful to the two insurance companies that cover my bank loans and lines of credit. They just stepped up to the plate after the forms were sent in and I explained my situation to them. Canada Life and Bankers Insurance of Florida have been exemplary. Again, since I made the decision to turn my will and life over and use the Eight Steps I am being supplied with all the things that are necessary for me to live my life today.

What is amazing to me is how I am being supplied with what I need in order to survive. Yes, I have to draw on my savings, but I have savings. Those savings were a direct result of turning my will and life over to the care of the Master Mind some years ago and asking for help. It is so interesting to me since that very black day back at the end of July when I decided to close my business down. I was despondent, and it felt like my life was ending. It was like a death to me. The sorrow was overwhelming as were the endless rejections. What a time that was. I am so grateful for my friends. If you don't have friends at this stage of your life, you need to make some very, very quickly. They are out there waiting to talk to you too, especially if you carry a positive message. A Master Mind group will create the environment for you to have a covenant that you can trust. You do have to believe that you can be guided to your greatest good, regardless of what your current financial or emotional circumstances are today. Believe me, they will change. We can't give up one day too soon. I have just experienced this in spades. One of my early problems (and probably why I wasted so many years) was I wouldn't enter into a covenant with the Master Mind about anything except drinking. I mentioned earlier when it came to relationships my attitude was, "Hold on, I'll handle that if you don't mind. Business. Whoa! Business is my territory." Well, not anymore.

The Gift of Families

I'm so grateful that I did ask for help from my family. My youngest daughter recently told me "We won the Dad lottery with you." I just got goose bumps writing this. It was so nice to hear.

Overcoming Adversity

A year ago this past July, I made the decision to surrender my life completely to the care and guidance of my Higher Power. I had no idea it would lead me here today. At that point in my life, I was in the midst of editing three shows, and we were on fire creatively. However, the shows we were finishing were started right around the time of the assault. For the better part of that year after we delivered the completed shows every single pitch we did was rejected.

Words cannot express how depressing and difficult it was to experience that kind of a disappointment because I honestly believed the ideas were good ones, and only time will tell if I was correct.

I was in a state of real despair and hopelessness. I never thought I would feel normal again. I never thought I would be happy or have any degree of peace in my life.

Here I am sixteen months after making that fateful decision to trust in a Higher Power completely, and the ship is turning around. Not as David Brady Productions, which is on life support, but as David Brady, author, lecturer, seminar leader, and speaker on "Aging, Finding Peace of Mind and Prosperity in the Second Half of Life." I feel that this step is working and that my covenant with my Master Mind is coming true, and I am being supplied with an abundance of all I need to live my life.

As a result of this reinvention of myself, I'm feeling peaceful, which is hard to believe. "Peaceful" is not how I would have described myself a few months ago. Not even a few weeks ago.

Today, I have enough. I have enough money for my current payables. I have enough emotional stability to let go of fear, worry, and resentment (most of the time).

I am off to a faculty meeting this afternoon at 4:45. But first I am completing the final revisions to this manuscript. I had a goal of finishing this book by September 30, 2013, but at least it is almost completed. I'm getting very close to the end. Since I started this book, a lot has changed, and I might say for the better emotionally.

I actually feel the excitement again. And I really thought all of that had gone from my life. I had a good conversation with my buddy, Bruce, yesterday. He's fighting the good fight with MS. He hopes to come out from Ontario and visit me, and I'm looking forward to that. He's going to travel with a young lady or two who will help him out of his wheelchair. They are friends of ours.

I have enough food in my fridge to eat healthy and balanced meals. I get pretty tired of my cooking or not cooking. My friends would burst out laughing at my referencing cooking when it seems that all I eat is fresh fruit and salads with nuts, skim milk (okay with cocoa in it) and really plain chicken, steak, or potatoes. I think it's my lack of culinary horizons that have caused me the loss of my real true romances in life.

One of the big concerns I have at this moment is the sale of my house. It is still on the market. However, I have to believe that I am being guided to the best possible outcome if it has not sold yet and there has to be a good reason for that. I'm now coming to see more than ever, that when things don't unfold as I think they should, there always seems to be something better coming down the road for me. I can never see it at the time, however.

As an example, potential relationships. I honestly don't know whether to give up in this area and call it a day or keep an open mind. You would think that, after two marriages, a failed near death experience and the loss of what had been arguably the best relationship of my life, I'd say, "Okay, that's it. The monk's life for me."

I think that when we have a busy family life with our adult children and our grandkids, it will take care of a lot of emotional needs. When I don't have that kind of interaction (because my older adult children are extremely busy and living in two countries), it doesn't afford me that opportunity.

My two youngest children are 25 and 24. Not the age where they want to be hanging out with Dad, if you catch my drift. Not that they don't love hanging out with me at times. They do. In fact, as I sit here editing this, my son Brendan and his girlfriend Cailin are here vising and have been here with me for the past week; it has been wonderful. We will celebrate Brendan's 25th birthday tomorrow, October 9th, by having dinner at the top of Grouse Mountain. The next day he and Cailin will drive back to Toronto. How lucky am I to be able to do this with my son and his girlfriend? I would say very lucky, indeed, as a family is the most important gift we will ever have in our lives.

This realization about family is something that took a very long time for me to learn. As this step suggests, I try to be a powerful example to both of them that having faith is working in my life. .

Living Alone But Not Lonely

When you are on your own, life feels different. I am currently spending a lot of time alone. I have no television and only Netflix on my computer. Fortunately, I love to read. My new apartment in West Vancouver is sparsely furnished as I await the sale of my furnished home in Ontario. Consequently, I have very little in my place except for two chairs and a bed from IKEA. As a result, this apartment is like a monk's quarters, which given my relationship status, may be quite appropriate! Very Zen. I brought some posters from my Toronto residence/edit suite that remind me of my past successes. Right across from the chair I'm sitting in is the poster of *The Grey Fox* and next to it a full-page article from the *Vancouver Province*, written in 1980. There is a picture of my late business associate, Phillip Borsos, with the headline, "Borsos Shooting Miner's Tale." I have the poster for *Yonge Street, Toronto Rock & Roll Stories*, a series that we produced for CTV/Bravo! with an article from the *National Post* newspaper. Next to it is another poster of my last production of "Super Volcano, Yellowstone's Fury" for *Doc Zone* that is scheduled to air in 2014 on the Smithsonian Channel in the United States.

Beside that poster of *Yonge Street* are two covers from the *Toronto Star*'s weekly TV listings about one of our productions, which aired on CBC and HD Net in the United States.

Remember the Covenant and My Mercedes?

By the way, I just got a call from the mechanic. Instead of $4,000, the bill will be roughly $600 to fix my Turbo Charger. Does this prove Master Mind's existence, or that I have a covenant because I prayed and released the outcome to Its guidance? It clearly didn't hurt. It does further affirm that if I continue to believe, trust, and ask for guidance, I get it. I can also even ask for help around money because I do want to pay off all my current creditors and investors.

What I Would Like To Do

I also want to be of service with my writing and speaking. What I do know is that if my heart is in the right place, there is no doubt in my mind that I will be guided to the right outcome.

Risk Failure

Today I had a chance to guide my students through an exercise in class. The purpose was to point out how important it is to take risks and to risk failure. Those crushing defeats I had in the past have been the very catalysts that have generated the greatest positive changes in my life. It's important to risk letting go of perfectionism and fear and to embrace change. These qualities apply to all our lives regardless of our age. We have to be willing to put ourselves out there. If we think about it, what have we really got to lose?

We're all headed for the departure lounge at some point. Do we want to get there and say, "Damn, why didn't I say hello to that person?

Why didn't I try and write my memoirs? Why didn't I tell my spouse how much I loved her? Why didn't I tell my children how important they were to me and that I loved them? Why didn't I ski that double black diamond run? Why didn't I get a new Triumph Bonneville when I wanted to?"

Furthermore, why didn't I forgive my friend for hurting my feelings all those years ago? It's so long ago I can't even remember why I got angry. Why haven't I spoken to them in years? My mind says, "I'm not going to be the one to pick up the phone." PICK IT UP before it's too late. Take a chance. Risk failure. Risk rejection. Risk success. If you find yourself in a place of depression or loneliness, then it's imperative to reach out to others. It is often said that there is always someone in worse shape than you, so reach out to them too. Volunteer at a soup kitchen for the homeless. Help other seniors who are unable to leave their homes or apartments. Try helping out with Meals on Wheels. There are so many great opportunities out there for all of us to be of service.

Have you always been interested in creative endeavors? Join the local amateur theater, writing group, poetry enthusiasts, or fine arts group. Initially, you may feel nervous if you don't know anyone. Can you remember when you were anxious and shy on your first day of school? Oh my, how we worried about being judged because we were so self-conscious of our age, physique, looks, or histories. Some of us just lacked the core confidence to get out there.

If we have a Master Mind group, we are blessed and thus able to get active in some ways. It gives us all a chance to be of service. True happiness does come from being of service. What about living in a manner that sets the highest example for those around you? Have you ever noticed those folks that are always happy regardless of their circumstances? They are powerful examples to us as of how to act. If we are chronically unhappy mature men and women, people will run from us like the plague. Who wants to be around someone who is negative, judgmental, full of self-pity, and mean? Not me. Here is a quote from a friend of mine who is a physician, a brilliant screenwriter, and whose spiritual guru said to him in the depths of his existential angst, "You are drowning in your shit. You smell so bad that nobody wants to be around you."

I don't know how anyone could be clearer in their communication about their place in life when they are in that negative frame of mind. In honor of my friend Bill, I suggest we all continue to pray for humility. Humility is a wonderful gift and within it are the seeds of true happiness. For the third time, it's also imperative to have a gratitude list — just in case it didn't sink in the other two times (smiley face should be here). Regardless of where we are in our lives, and what difficulties we've had to face and or overcome, if we sit down and do an honest reflection with others, we will be able to look back on our lives and realize just how blessed we've been.

Proof of Faulty Filter and Imperfection

As I have previously shared with you, my faulty filter is one of my primary character defects. It turns out the building manager where I live has not painted the parking lot wall on the ground level for years. They painted it yesterday and removed all the reference numbers. I've been here and parking in the same spot about three weeks. I came out his morning to find a note on my car because I had apparently parked in the wrong location. The note was fairly lengthy and suggested that I didn't know that the parking was paid for and reserved.

I've been parking beside this car for the

past three weeks. The owner of the car doesn't live in my complex, but works at a retail store right next to the entrance to our parking lot. They can see that there are now no clear markings on the wall. How do I react? My first thought is to write them an equally moronic (in my opinion) note: "Dear Mr./Ms. Perfection. I aspire to be as intelligent as you one day. Wow, I'm so glad you were there to let me know that where I was parking was paid parking and reserved too. I would have thought these spaces were for residents of our complex — not sales associates — but, obviously I was just too dimwitted to realize that and I can't tell you how grateful I am that you pointed out my imperfection and lack of temporal and spatial cognitive skills. I grovel before your insight and wisdom. Please, please just go 'propagate' yourself and die!" Oops.

This is why I will share my story with you and not the driver. Hopefully, in spite of my lapse of judgment on my profanity, you will still find me a positive example, in spite of my obvious imperfections.

The fact is that I practiced humility and restraint of both pen and tongue, which is a positive step for me. I believe that it is progress, not perfection that we should be pursuing. Perfectionism is a major flaw that plagues so many of us and causes such pain.

Progress, Not Perfection

You would think after the previous paragraphs on how to clear out the faulty filter, practice humility and restraint of pen and tongue, I would sort of be a spiritual giant, wouldn't you? Well, guess what I just did (it really is progress not perfection)? In a moment devoid of any humility or sound judgment, I started to read an article by a well-known Canadian television journalist John Doyle. He is the television critic for Canada's national newspaper, *The Globe and Mail*. Now, I can't say that John is any great fan of mine, but on a few occasions he has spoken kindly about some of my productions. But I do love his writing. The article was about the sorry state of Canadian broadcasting and lamenting the race to the bottom (as it were — my words). He went on to point out the absolute mediocrity of the executives running Canadian broadcasting (and primarily the Canadian Broadcasting Corporation). In a moment of what I felt to be Divine Inspiration, I thought, what the hell. I should let the executive who turned down my series idea for CANUSA Lodge know what I really think of his abilities and skills. Then, with the trumpets and sirens of insanity screeching in my head, I thought, I might as well let the president and the new executive vice president of the CBC know just exactly how fed up I am. As far as I'm concerned, they should just go ahead and shut the whole bloated bureaucracy down. (In the background will be many conservatives howling with glee and hoping my message is heard. Members of the Conservative Party of Canada want desperately to shut down the CBC.)

My reasoning has primarily to do with the pursuit of creative excellence. CBC is not a commercial broadcaster. Needless to say, my friend and legal counsel for 30 years who read what I thought was a brilliant missive, said, "I just got a strong whiff of your bridge burning in Toronto even though you are sitting five thousand kilometers away in Vancouver." While my delivery lacked a certain degree of subtlety, I still stand by my comments.

However, since I wrote that piece above, CBC has made some good changes. In July 2015, Sally Catto was promoted to the position of general manager of television programing. And for me, a lot has gone on too. I let my friend who was brought on to take over CBC's documentary strand that I am as done as dinner. That it is over for me and producing. No more films or television shows. I don't want to see CBC shut down, even though they turned down four of my projects. Honest to God. (I will complete this thought in the epilogue.)

A Little Cheese with That Whine

Today is my second day out of bed. I got a very severe flu last Thursday night. That was a week ago today. I still got up Friday and went swimming again, but I didn't feel right. I went to meet some friends Saturday morning and worked with a fellow who asked me for help with his finances. We got together and talked about where he was in life. Then we looked at what steps he might take to start correcting his thinking and behavior around money and debiting.

As seniors (I hate that word), we need to

be aware of these respiratory illnesses. I can set an example for others by insuring I practice good self-care. I don't have anyone out here that I can call yet.

Fortunately, for me, my son Brendan arrived on Sunday night from Vancouver Island. He's now been with me for five days. That was a real blessing, and I was able to enjoy my time with him. I did try to get up and go to dinner with him, but all I did was cough up a storm and not enjoy any of my food. But it was nice to have him here.

What I notice when I get sick is that I don't do sick "well." I tend to be rather immature. If there is anyone around to listen, I willingly moan and groan about how bad I feel. I don't know if it's a "male" thing or what.

Do you find it hard to ask anyone for guidance when you're sick too? My conscious contact seems to evaporate. Do you struggle with prayer and meditation? It doesn't really come too easily to me in this state, even in the best of times. As I may have indicated in the past, I have a mind that is rather quick. I use to say, "I even sleep fast." My mind just spins at a very high RPM. The trouble is that sometimes it doesn't go anywhere, except when it tells me, "Okay, this is it. You're on the way out. You know you have the new MERS (replacing SARS). And by the way, that pneumonia shot you paid two or three hundred bucks for didn't work." My mind just goes to worst-case scenario-zing and catastrophizes. It is often my default setting

Not to beat an idea to death, but my mind is like one of those restaurant wheels where the waiter places the order, and the chef then turns the wheel endlessly to read the next slip. My mind is analogous to that wheel and just keeps spinning and looking to the next thought to worry about. I can ask the Master Mind's guidance and just chill out and wait for answers to materialize. I'm learning that I need to be patient. The Master Mind is not a short-order cook — well, not for me at least.

If we are open to the Master Mind, then many wonderful things seem to come our way. All my disability insurance claims have now been approved. My car is fixed. My son is here. I am at peace 90% of the time. I seem to be doing well in most areas of my life. What I need to do is lock down my formal Master Mind group.

Master Mind Success

Saturday, October 18, 2013

We had our first Master Mind meeting this morning. There were three of us — Mike, Jey, and me.

Try, Try Again

I submitted some new projects to broadcasters over the past two months. As of last week (second week of January 2014), they were all turned down. I do feel a sense of acceptance now that my days of producing network television appear to be over. I trust that I am being guided to the best outcome. I choose to no longer hold false hope that this area of my life is going to change. It's not worth the emotional turmoil I keep going through in submitting these ideas and then being rejected. Regardless of that news, I do feel a peace of mind because of the Eight Steps.

Hope Springs Eternal

I am beginning to feel a renewed sense of hope. I know from first-hand experience that I do have a message of hope to share with others. I intend to use that gift of writing and speaking to be of service and to assist others like myself who have found themselves at a turning point in life and are not certain which path to follow.

I want to tell all of you about an amazing therapy I am doing called neurofeedback.

Neurofeedback is a type of biofeedback that measures brain waves to produce a signal that can be used as feedback on brain activity to teach self-regulation.

Neurofeedback is commonly provided using video or sound, with positive feedback for desired brain activity and negative feedback for brain activity that is undesirable. The most accurate form of neurofeedback is the one guided by EEG that is usually used in clinical settings.

What I do is see a clinician, Linda Bailey, who is a Registered Nurse and works out of a clinic in North Vancouver. The neuroscientists, who created the program, trained Linda. My analogy for neurofeedback is that it is like using the disk repair tool on my Mac Book Air. That software repairs the damaged files on the hard drive. In this case, my hard drive is analogous to my brain, and the neurofeedback is repairing and rebooting my brain.

I have now undergone 83 sessions. As a result of this therapy, I have been able to cease taking all of my medications. My anxiety level has dropped significantly. I can focus better. I am just so grateful that my friend Richard led me to this. He was in my Master Mind group in Ontario. Richard used neurofeedback to overcome post-traumatic stress disorder. As a result of the neurofeedback, I would say that right here, right now I feel peace of mind, and you can too.

I can now also focus on producing my video talks — corporate, inspirational, motivational, and spiritual. This is something I've always wanted to do. I have spoken to my associates at the university and they are going to help me out with two cameras, and two of the students in cinematography will shoot this for me. I've spoken to a few of my screenwriting students who will act as my crew. I am back to film production 101, where I started 30 years ago.

To Wrap Up Our Journey

Could I have planned this? I'm not sure whether I could have ever dreamt of something like this happening. It is literally like a Hollywood movie with a happy ending. I will have to let you know how it works out financially, but I know that I have enough for today.

What I have learned through this journey that I've just taken is that I do have value as a human being. If we ask for help and we do let go of old self-defeating thinking and beliefs about ourselves, we will get it. I have also learned that I am a long way from perfection and that I really need to learn to love myself, warts and all. I also believe that prosperity includes the richness of family and friends and a relationship with a Higher Power of your choice. All the money in the world is meaningless if we don't have someone to share it with.

It is my sincere belief that you too will find

whatever it is you are looking for if you will follow these simple Eight Steps.

I want to thank you personally for investing your money in buying this book and for taking the time to read it, and I pray you will find all the happiness and purpose you have been seeking for in your own life. I would love to hear from any of you if you are willing to contact me and let me know about your journey. You can email me at davidbradybooks@gmail.com

It is my heartfelt prayer that each and every one of you will be guided to the greatest good that you could have ever hoped for and that you too will find the way to overcome adversity, find peace of mind, prosperity, and a conscious contact with the Master Mind of your choice, who will supply you with everything you need to live your life as you always desired.

Epilogue: July 25, 2016

One year ago I thought I had permanently shut down my production company. I did shut down my operations in Sandhurst, Ontario. I've now moved our offices to Toronto and Vancouver. I will leave in three weeks to travel to Nashville to speak to an author about 24 of her books that we may try to adapt for a streaming series.

She is an amazing writer and has sold between 70 and 90 million books, depending on who you speak with or where you look. They were written to be adapted to the screen. And they are remarkable stories about women exacting justice for other women who have been mistreated, abused, or harmed. Justice without pointless violence, but brilliant and fun "paybacks." And the men in the books are not all two-dimensional cartoon characters. The men who help her small cadre of friends are both entertaining and intelligent, as well as empathetic to the women's cause.

I just completed my third book, *Reflections on Money, Sex & Power: How to Use Them, Not Abuse and Enjoy Them in Your Life*. I've made the decision to speak and write about the three books I have now written, which cover the topics of childhood trauma; finding and enjoying real success, peace, and true happiness in life; and reflections on how to give boomers a real reason to get up in the morning and just not sit around waiting to die. Life is way too short to hit the pause button. Everything I am doing is based on what I've learned since I began this book over three years ago.

I have now had over 100,00 views of my two YouTube videos, *Aging With Dignity, Living With Grace* and *Transforming Childhood Trauma*. I have 37 reviews; 35 of them are 5 out of 5 stars. Thank you all.

I have two wonderful editors: one out of New York City who is editing both my *Transforming Childhood Trauma* and *Reflections on Money, Sex & Power*, and another out of Toronto who has helped me revise this book.

Words cannot express the incredible journey that I've been on over the past 36 months here in Vancouver and back in Toronto.

I had moved over to Kit's Point in Kitsilano. It gives me an even more beautiful view of the Pacific Ocean and the ships in the harbor, and I can look back at picturesque West Vancouver.

However, my heart lies on the North Shore and I am now first in line to get one of the beautiful historic cottages in Horseshoe Bay, in West Vancouver. It is stunningly beautiful there. Most of my social life in Vancouver is on the North Shore and I'm looking forward to being able to move back to the area.

The great news is that a significant part of

my brain injury has healed. Miracles do happen. I took lemons and made lemonade.

I will now focus on writing and speaking to others, including anyone who has suffered a life-altering event, as well as to seniors and boomers about overcoming adversity and finding peace of mind and prosperity, regardless of where you are in life. I intend to do one-day seminars that are focused on finding a spiritual solution to all of our problems in life. First up in the schedule will be anyone who has ever suffered from child abuse and is looking for a solution. Then I will speak to boomers about rebooting their lives and finding real peace and purpose again. Third up will be my book *Reflections on Money, Sex & Power* for those who truly want success — and by that I mean great personal relationships that work, financial stability, and a new relationship with a Power Greater Than Themselves that is not dogmatically based nor dependent on specific theology, in case you are not associated with any formal or traditional faith. To me the most precious gift I've found is that one that grants us all the peace of mind that really does surpass understanding.

In other good news, I began my coaching work with Steve Harrison and his brother Bill at Bradley Communications in Philadelphia. I am attending their National Publicity Summit in New York City from October 26 to October 29 this coming fall. Bradley Communications is the marketing and advertising powerhouse behind Jack Canfield and Mark Victor Hansen's *Chicken Soup for the Soul* franchise, as well as such notable books as *Rich Dad, Poor Dad* and *Men Are From Mars, Women Are From Venus*.

It is my goal to join those gentlemen and I aspire to also be a best-selling author as a result of my relationship with them.

Only time will tell, so let's watch and see

what happens. If you are having any difficulties in your life today, please remember that there is a solution. To find a Master Mind group, look for a Unity Church or Spiritual Center, Community Center, or Google Master Mind groups. There are Master Mind groups for business, spirituality, and health, and all you have to do is look for them online.

Thanks to each and every one of you who has taken the time to get this far and for allowing me to share my journey with you. I pray I've not appeared too arrogant or grandiose, it's just that this has been my journey and my story. It is my sincere hope that anything I've written here has been of some help to you, the reader. I would also ask that if you enjoyed the book to please go to Amazon.com and give it a review. If you dislike it, please email and tell me what you didn't like about it. I am always open to suggestions and feedback.

Kind regards and much love from beautiful Vancouver, British Columbia.

davidbradybooks@gmail.com

Made in the USA
Lexington, KY
25 August 2019